Study Daniel:

15 Lessons On

God's Enduring

Kingdom

Jason Dexter
Author and General Editor

Study Daniel: 15 Lessons on God's Enduring Kingdom
Copyright © 2022 by Jason Dexter
All rights reserved

D1328421

Study and Obey

Table of Contents

Daniel 1

Outline

I. The background: Defeat to Babylon (1-2)
II. The subjects: young men with no blemish (3-4)
III. The plan: brainwashing (5-7)
IV. The resolve: No compromise! (8)
V. The request: A test (9-13)
VI. The result: Success (14-16)
VII. The verdict: These men were wiser than all the rest of Babylon (17-21)

I. The background: Defeat to Babylon (1-2)

Background Discussion Questions:

- Why was Jerusalem being attacked?
- What happened to Judea after this?
- Who won the battle? Why?
- What do you know about the empire of Babylon?
- What did Nebuchadnezzar do after he defeated Jerusalem? Why?
- What does the exile teach us about God's character?

Cross-References

2 Kings 24-25 – These chapters give the history of three Babylonian assaults against Jerusalem.

Isaiah 39:6-7 –Behold, the days are coming, when all that is in your house, and that which your fathers have stored up till this day, shall be carried to Babylon. Nothing shall be left, says the Lord.

Ezekiel 14:20, 28:3 – Daniel was mentioned by Ezekiel as being extraordinarily wise and righteous. A real person.

Hebrews 12:1 - For the moment all discipline seems painful rather than pleasant, but later it yields the peaceful fruit of righteousness to those who have been trained by it.

Teaching Points

1. Repeated warnings - For decades, prophets had been warning Judah that God would punish her for her gross sins and rebellion against the Lord. In recent years, these warnings reached a fever pitch. However, Judah did not listen. The prophets were ignored, scoffed at, or even thrown into prison and cut in two. God planned to use 70 years of captivity to bring the people to their knees and turn them back to Himself. Although His judgment was severe, He still never forgot His promises to David and always preserved a remnant of the nation and a remnant who was faithful to himself.

Sin comes with consequences. God had promised Israel great blessings and prosperity if they were faithful. He also warned them about the results of disobedience. Though they were given a clear choice between the two paths (Deuteronomy 28), with the destination of each foretold, they still chose rebellion.

Reflect: Why, after experiencing God's discipline in their history so often, did they still rebel?

2. His chosen instrument was Babylon. The prophet Habakkuk was confused about how God, who is infinitely holy, could use an evil kingdom like Babylon to punish Judah (Habakkuk 1-2). Wasn't Judah, though still sinful, better than Babylon?

God's answer was that He would use Babylon for this purpose and one day, they too would experience judgment. When you look at the history of Babylon, it is easy to see God's sovereign hand.

They were just a small group of people with little influence and a small kingdom. But somehow, they suddenly rose to prominence and took over much of the known world. Their rise was rapid, and their downfall was equally quick.

Right before the seventy-year exile was up, they were miraculously defeated and conquered in one night. It is clear that God's sovereign hand was behind their rise and fall. They were unknowing and unwilling instruments in His hands.

Looking at history, you can see many times God has used even wicked nations to accomplish his purposes. One recent example is Nazi Germany. This evil regime rose to power quickly. Though they were horribly cruel, God did use the war they inflicted on Europe to drive the Jews out of the places they had taken root for nearly two thousand years, bringing them back again to populate Israel.

Reflect: What do we learn from this about God's sovereignty?

Babylon conquered Jerusalem and Judah three times, each time taking captive more of the population. After each of the first two times, Judah rebelled again, only to be defeated.

Daniel and his friends were taken in the first group. At that time, only some of the nobility were taken.

We will see that Nebuchadnezzar is a crucial character in this book and God will do great work in his life. His name means "Nebo is the protector against misfortune." Nebuchadnezzar took the temple treasuries from Jerusalem to his own temple as a kind of war prize to show the superiority of his gods, when actually, the one true God gave him victory.

For decades, critics found fault with the Bible, saying that other historical sources did not record Nebuchadnezzar as practicing this.

However, as is often the case, the Bible critics were proved wrong as inscriptions were found ascribing this very practice to him.

II. The subjects: young men with no blemish (3-4)

Discussion Questions

- What kind of people did Nebuchadnezzar take back to Babylon? Why?

Cross-References

Proverbs 22:6 - Train up a child in the way he should go; even when he is old he will not depart from it.

Teaching Points

1. A group of Judean youths was taken - No one knows the exact number taken captive, but it was apparently a large-sized group. The word "youth" is usually used in Scripture to denote young men between fourteen and eighteen. We also know that Daniel lived at least seventy-five years after this, so that age frame fits. Also, it fits with the purpose of taking these young men as the powers to be would expect that the young would be easier to indoctrinate.

They were physically and mentally the cream of the crop. Each one was handsome, fit, and strong, with good posture and bearing. These young men excelled in all types of academics. But they weren't only skillful in studies; they displayed real-world wisdom to solve problems and exceptional discernment. However, they weren't nerds. Social grace and adept communication were also their strong suits. Only the best and the brightest were taken.

III. The plan: brainwashing (5-7)

Discussion Questions
- What was to happen after they were taken?
- Were they allowed to keep their Jewish identity?
- In what ways did Nebuchadnezzar try to brainwash them?
- What did he offer them as enticements to join his ranks?
- What are some ways that the world seeks to influence and mold young minds today?
- Why would it be difficult for youth in that situation to resist?
- What temptations to be conformed to the world might a young person face today?
- What advice would you give to youth about how to stand firm?
- What did the names mean that were given to Daniel and his friends?

- Why do you think the other Judean youths who were taken captive are not mentioned?

Cross-References

Proverbs 23:1-3 - When you sit down to eat with a ruler, observe carefully what is before you, and put a knife to your throat if you are given to appetite. Do not desire his delicacies, for they are deceptive food.

Romans 12:2 - Do not be conformed to this world, but be transformed by the renewal of your mind, that by testing you may discern what is the will of God, what is good and acceptable and perfect.

Colossians 2:8 - See to it that no one takes you captive by philosophy and empty deceit, according to human tradition, according to the elemental spirits of the world, and not according to Christ.

Teaching Points

1. Babylon wanted administrators it could control – The exiled youth were not to be prisoners. Neither were they slaves. The Babylonian government correctly realized that they had great potential. A willing servant is far more valuable than a slave.

The Babylonian kingdom needed people like this to serve as sub-rulers over their people and areas, administrative puppets, if you will. They were going to go through a three-year assimilation program at the University of Babylon. They were to learn the language, history, literature, and religion of the Chaldeans, while also learning to conform to the native lifestyle.

In the book of Exodus, Israel's Egyptian overlords offered them a stick. "Make bricks or we will beat you." Here, the gracious and benevolent Babylonians offered a carrot. "We will give you a good life, nice food, plenty of money, a steady job, an opportunity for promotion, and a position of power. You will be better off than your kinsmen back in Judah."

This plan was ingenious:

A. Take the young, who are more impressionable.
B. Remove them from their mentors, who could positively influence them.
C. Isolate them in a foreign environment.

7

D. Give them free education, teach them, train them, and make them feel indebted.

E. Give them good food and tempt them with the riches and power that could be theirs.

F. Wipe out all vestiges of their past belief and practice by giving them new names.

This plan was well-thought and well-executed. In most cases, it must have worked to perfection. The program would allow the Babylonians to make use of not only the natural resources of other countries but also the human resources and turn the leaders of those countries slowly in favor of Babylon. It is the same type of information propaganda practiced by many regimes in history. If you can change their minds to accept you, you don't have to fight them.

Daniel lived in a place that had no respect for God. There were temptations all around him. The education system was brainwashing people to believe in lies instead of the truth from God. There was tremendous pressure to conform to society and be like everyone else.

We also live in a society that does not honor God. The education system, not only here but around the world, brainwashes people to accept lies, including evolution and atheism. There is intense pressure to conform and be like everyone else.

The next step was to change their names. Here are their previous names and meaning and their new names and meaning.

Belteshazzar –It was changed from "God is my judge" to "Bel, protect the king."

Shadrach – It was changed from "The Lord is gracious" to "Command of Aku."

Meshach – It was changed from "Who is like the Lord" to "who is what Aku is."

Abed-nego – It was changed from "The Lord is my helper" to "servant of Nebo."

Application: The world will seek to pressure you to compromise. You need to be alert (1 Peter 5:8) to discern from where the attack is coming. Not every promotion should be accepted, and not every lucrative job offer is the one God has for you. Do not love the world or the things in the world because these things fade away while God's Word stands forever.

IV. The resolve: No compromise! (8)

Discussion Questions

- At what point did Daniel draw the line?
- Why did he draw the line here?
- What does this tell us about his character?
- What does this tell us about his relationship with the Lord?
- Do you think most kids growing up in Christian families today would take that kind of a stand?
- How can you decide where to draw the line and where accommodation is acceptable?
- Share a testimony about a time you have been pressured to do something wrong. What lessons did you learn from it?
- Would it have been wrong for Daniel to eat this food? Why or why not?

Cross-References

Psalms 119:106 - I have sworn an oath and confirmed it, to keep your righteous rules.

Psalms 119:115 - Depart from me, you evildoers, that I may keep the commandments of my God.

Teaching Points

1. Daniel made up his mind not to defile himself -

Daniel 1:8 - *But Daniel resolved that he would not defile himself with the king's food, or with the wine that he drank. Therefore he asked the chief of the eunuchs to allow him not to defile himself.*

This is the key verse in the whole chapter. It highlights one aspect of Daniel's character that will show itself throughout the book. That is his resolve. He made up his mind that he would not defile himself.

What a powerful statement this is. We see the might and strategies of the Babylonian ruler on one side. On the other side, we see a teenage boy. He is far from home, lonely, and surrounded by pagan culture. Temptations and sin are on every side. And when he is faced with a temptation, he draws a line in his mind and resolves that he will not cross it.

He was commanded to eat this food. Why would he refuse? He did not object to the schooling, and there is no record of objection to his name change. Both of these things were external and neither was technically forbidden in the Mosaic law. He did refuse to eat the food. In Leviticus 11:4-20, there is a list of foods that were unlawful for Jews to eat. Some include pigs, eels, ravens, camels, and bats. While wine was not expressly forbidden, it was warned against (Proverbs 23:31-35).

Notice where Daniel drew his line in the sand. It was not based on his own opinion, tradition, customs, or culture. It is based on the Word of God. God's Word clearly forbids him from eating this food, so he resolved not to. He made up his mind to do what was right without compromise and without offering excuses.

Even in the face of overwhelming pressure, he stood on the truth and wouldn't budge.

Exodus 23:2 says, *"Do not follow the crowd in doing wrong."*

He didn't.

Was this an easy decision for Daniel? I am sure he knew that the potential consequence of disobedience was death. What use would the king have for captives who wouldn't obey?

The results were less important to him than the principle. He made up his mind to do what was right without compromise and without offering excuses.

Scores of people I have met, if they were in that situation, would have said, "I have to do it." There is no choice, right?

You are all alone in a foreign country under the rule of pagans. They hold your life in their hands, seemingly. But while it may seem like resistance is futile, it's not.

Daniel had a choice. We all have a choice. We never have to do wrong. Wow, the world desperately needs this kind of believer! We must ask ourselves, what would we do if we were in Daniel's situation? Would we have given in?

Application: Let Daniel be an inspiration to all of us to stand uncompromisingly on the truth even in the face of powerful pressure to give in to the world's way. If we only learn this one lesson from this book, it will be well worth it.

V. The request: A test (9-13)

Discussion Questions

- How did Daniel handle this issue? What was his attitude?
- What did he propose?
- What do you think the other Israel youths would have thought of his chances for success?
- What are some "reasonable" excuses or justifications he could have come up with for why it was acceptable to compromise?
- Was he successful on the first try? What did he do when his first try failed?
- Daniel didn't offer excuses or justifications for eating the food. He could have made a lot. Like what?

Cross-References

James 3:17 - But the wisdom from above is first pure, then peaceable, gentle, open to reason, full of mercy and good fruits, impartial and sincere.

Luke 21:15 - For I will give you a mouth and wisdom, which none of your adversaries will be able to withstand or contradict.

Teaching Points

1. Daniel did not make excuses to justify compromise –

Many in Daniel's position would have compromised and then justified it.

'Possible excuses include:

- God abandoned me in this foreign country. Maybe He isn't real, or perhaps I don't need to serve Him anymore.
- I have no choice. If I don't eat it, they will kill me.
- Perhaps I am willing to die for it, but if I don't eat it, they will get angry with all of us Judah boys, and then I will be responsible for the punishment the rest of them receive.
- It's not really that big of a deal. It's only food. God knows my heart.
- God must have brought me here for a reason. He wants me to be an influence for Him. If I don't fit in, I will never have the position or the opportunity to influence others for Him.
- Once I get to power, I can use my influence for Him.

2. Daniel did exercise wisdom in the way he stood his ground –

Reflect: What would have happened if Daniel had made an excuse and eaten the food?

We wouldn't even have the book of Daniel. Eating the food would be the first foot going down the slippery slope. One compromise would have led to another, and Daniel would have been just one more of the flattering, manipulative wise men we will see around the king's court later in this book.

Let's look at how he handled the situation. Although he made up his mind, he didn't just flaunt it in the official's face and arrogantly declare that he wouldn't do it. He didn't say, "Old Neb can stuff the food in his own fat face for all I care; I'm not going to eat it."

He displayed:

Humility – He asked for permission.

Wisdom – He proposed a test. He knew how the world works, and it is geared towards results. He proposed a solution that would be acceptable on all sides.

Faith – He had faith that God would make the test work.

Perseverance – When the first guy rejected him, he didn't give up but went and asked another guy.

We can learn a lot from this passage about how to solve problems. When the world tempts us, too often we simply just give in. Other times we respond with rude arrogance and flaunt our "righteousness" in their face.

Instead, we can think of a proposal that will work to all sides' satisfaction. We can try to stand firmly on the Word of God without offending others. Sure, this will not "work" every time. If they don't listen to reason, we still do need to do what is right, even if that is offensive. But if we take a humble, respectful attitude and ask for permission or propose another solution, many problems will be solved before reaching the "I quit" or "just kill me" stage.

Proverbs 2:6 - *For the Lord gives wisdom; from his mouth come knowledge and understanding.*

Application: Do you need special wisdom for a situation that you are facing? Ask the Lord. He will give you discernment as you seek His will.

God gives the wisdom to solve problems. Go to Him for it.

VI. The result: Success (14-16)

Discussion Questions

- Why was he successful in the end?
- Was it a natural or supernatural explanation?

Cross-References

Genesis 39:21 - But the Lord was with Joseph and showed him steadfast love and gave him favor in the sight of the keeper of the prison.

Psalms 4:3 - But know that the LORD has set apart the godly for himself; the LORD hears when I call to him.

Proverbs 16:7 - When a man's ways please the Lord, he makes even his enemies to be at peace with him.

Haggai 1:6 - You have sown much, and harvested little. You eat, but you never have enough; you drink, but you never have your fill. You clothe yourselves, but no one is warm. And he who earns wages does so to put them into a bag with holes.

Matthew 4:4 - But he answered, "It is written, "'Man shall not live by bread alone, but by every word that comes from the mouth of God.'"

Teaching Points

1. God made them appear healthier after ten days – If we stand firm on His Word and take a "leap of faith," He will honor that. That doesn't mean we will get what we want every time.

Sometimes persecution or trouble will still come. Nonetheless, the Lord is with us, and if it is His will for us to succeed, He will bring it about no matter what. God looks out for those who belong to Him.

2. The Daniel de-tox – Many people have unhealthy eating habits. The Babylonian court encouraged them. Unhealthy eating habits have an adverse effect on our health, mental and physical. Vegetables and fruit have always been the healthiest foods. The Bible teaches that you "reap what you sow." It is also true with the foods we eat. If you eat more nutritious foods, you will be healthier.

Some believers have suggested a ten-day "Daniel de-tox" as a way to clear out toxins from our system and go back to the basics. Many who have tried it have found inflammation down and energy levels up.

Application: Consider your eating habits. Are you honoring God with your body as a temple for Him? Are you losing self-control and allowing the world to tempt you with delicacies that are harming your health? God wants us to honor Him with our bodies. The longer we live, the longer we can serve Him and our families. Move more. Eat better. Many scientific studies equate those two simple concepts with a longer and healthier life. The Bible already taught these principles long ago (1 Corinthians 6:12-20).

VII. The verdict: These men were wiser than all the rest of Babylon (17-21)

Discussion Questions

- What position did they get after this education period was over?

Teaching Points

1. They were promoted!

In verse 17, God blesses these four young men's obedience. He gives them great skill, knowledge, and wisdom, blessing them with special gifts and abilities. The Bible says that He who is faithful in a little thing is also faithful in much. They had proven their obedience to God in this "little thing" in front of some low-ranking officials. And because of that, they would have many more opportunities to use their gifts and talents to serve God in kingdom-altering events.

We see in verses 18-20 that they have an audience with the king. That audience likely came after the three years of their education program were up. And the king was very impressed by their wisdom and understanding.

An objective observer would conclude that not eating the food would destroy their political careers and possibly their lives. But amazingly, doing what seemed like political suicide from man's perspective was the catalyst that sparked their rise to political office.

Not everything is always what it seems. We don't have to do things the world's way. People think conforming to culture is the only way to get results, but it is a lie. Being bold, truthful, and full of integrity often brings more long-term results. Bosses often appreciate it when they realize they are dealing with a person of integrity who will not cheat them or compromise their beliefs.

Application: We live in a dark and pagan world like Daniel. The truth of God has been exchanged for a lie. The world around us tries to squeeze us into its mold, just as it did with Daniel. We are constantly tempted and pressured to give in and be the same as everyone else, and we are tempted to compromise what we know is right.

Perhaps in the past you have faced this pressure. Perhaps in the past you gave in. But today, you have a choice. Will you be like Daniel and resolve to do what is right no matter what?

Philippians 2:15 - *That you may be blameless and innocent, children of God without blemish in the midst of a crooked and twisted generation, among whom you shine as lights in the world.*

Daniel 2:1-18

Outline

I. The setting: Nebuchadnezzar's dream (1)
II. The inability and political jostling of his "wise" men (2-12)
III. Daniel wisely makes a request for time and then seeks the Lord (13-18)
IV. Daniel praises the Lord after the dream is revealed (19-23)
V. Daniel gives credit to the Lord for the interpretation (24-30)
VI. The king's dream revealed (31-35)
VII. The interpretation of the king's dream (36-45)
VIII. Daniel is rewarded (46-49)

I. The setting: Nebuchadnezzar's dream (1)

Cross-references

Genesis 40 – God gives Pharaoh a dream and Joseph the interpretation to help protect Israel and vault Joseph into power.

Jeremiah 27:5 - It is I who by my great power and my outstretched arm have made the earth, with the men and animals that are on the earth, and I give it to whomever it seems right to me.

Teaching Points

1. There is some difficulty with the date of this account. It is said to be "in the second year of the reign of Nebuchadnezzar." But presumably, Daniel was already in Babylon for three years by this point (Daniel 1:5).

How then could this happen in the second year?

Here are a couple of possibilities:

- Perhaps, though three years were appointed for the education of other youth, Daniel was such a quick learner that he "graduated" from this program before the three years were up.
- Another possibility is that this refers to the second year of Nebuchadnezzar's sole reign as king, while before this he co-reigned with his father for some time.

2. Nebuchadnezzar had a restless night filled with dreams – In verse 1, the dreams come first. And after that, his spirit becomes unsettled, and he can't sleep. The mystery and the magnitude of the dream bothered him. It seemed evident to him that this dream was not just an ordinary dream. It was meant to convey a message to him, but he couldn't understand it. That curiosity drove him to reach out to experts who could help decipher the puzzle.

II. The inability and political jostling of his "wise" men (2-12)

Discussion Questions

- What kind of people did Nebuchadnezzar call in to tell him his dream and interpret it?
- Why wouldn't he tell them the content of his dream?
- What do you notice about Nebuchadnezzar and all these wise men from this passage?
- Do you think Nebuchadnezzar was right in his accusations about their motives?
- Were they correct in verses 10-12?
- What does this tell us about the wise men's ability as sorcerers/magicians and false religious leaders?
- Why were they unable to tell him his dream?
- What does this tell us about the ability of these types of religious figures today?
- Nebuchadnezzar was brilliant. He knew the hearts of his supposed wise men and their political scheming. He wasn't in the dark about the corruption and deception. So why did he rely on these guys?

Cross-References

Proverbs 19:12 - A king's wrath is like the growling of a lion, but his favor is like dew on the grass.

Proverbs 20:2 - The terror of a king is like the growling of a lion; whoever provokes him to anger forfeits his life.

Isaiah 47:12-15 - Stand fast in your enchantments and your many sorceries, with which you have labored from your youth; perhaps you may be able to succeed; perhaps you may inspire terror. You are wearied with your many counsels; let them stand forth and save you, those who divide the heavens, who gaze at the stars, who at the new moons make known what shall come upon you. Behold, they are like stubble; the fire consumes them; they cannot deliver themselves from the power of the flame. No coal for warming oneself is this, no fire to sit before! Such to you are those with whom you have labored, who have done business with you from your youth; they wander about, each in his own direction; there is no one to save you.

Teaching Points

1. Nebuchadnezzar reached out to the "experts" for help –

He did not understand the meaning of the dream, and that really bothered him. In desperation, he turned to the only source of help he could find.

Nebuchadnezzar was familiar with their political maneuvering and knew their deception and trickery. From the text, it is clear that he did not trust them to give the correct interpretation. Instead, they would simply make up some vague story that sounded good and would be difficult to disprove.

Reflect - Since he knew their deceit and inability to solve this puzzle, why did he still rely on them?

Simply put, he had nowhere else to turn. He lived in a culture that was shrouded in darkness. False gods were worshiped in the form of idols. These were the religious leaders and wisest people in society. They were supposed to have the answers. Yet they were blind leaders of the blind.

On some level, the king knew that they were a farce and that what they were selling was a scam. But there seemed to be no other choices. These were the only people he could turn to, which is a sad state.

Application – It is essential to turn to the right people for counsel. Society has so-called experts from whom people tend to solicit help, including psychologists, self-help gurus, authors, and all manner of counselors. Many also look to their parents, neighbors, or co-workers for advice.

Proverbs 24:6 - *For by wise guidance you can wage your war, and in abundance of counselors there is victory.*

Counsel is easy to get, but we need to get it from the right source.

Proverbs 13:20 - *Whoever walks with the wise becomes wise,*
but the companion of fools will suffer harm.

If you ask an unbeliever for advice on a moral issue, know that it will come from a completely different worldview.

The simple lesson for us is this; ask mature, godly believers for advice.

2. Nebuchadnezzar knew how to deal with them – While he did look to them for aid out of necessity, he did not trust them.

He refused to tell them the contents of the dream to test if what they were speaking was really true. The test was simple. If they could reveal to him what he dreamt, the interpretation would be trustworthy. Having that special knowledge would validate their interpretation of the dream.

Any 10-year-old can come up with an interpretation for a dream, and a wise one would put its events far enough into the future that it couldn't be tested and proved wrong.

3. The wrath of Nebuchadnezzar – Nebuchadnezzar had been infected with power and grown extraordinarily prideful and arrogant. As the highest person on earth, he expected others to do his bidding and do it immediately. It didn't matter how absurd the request was; he demanded people do it.

Also, as we see later in the book, he makes a lot of threats. He has power and intends to use it. These threats are not idle either. He will follow through because he is a man of fury and wrath.

The king declared that if they were unable to reveal the contents of his dream, they would be "torn from limb to limb" and their "houses... laid

ruins." (Daniel 1:5) On the other hand, he was a nice guy. If they came through, there would be great personal reward.

When the wise men told him that this was impossible, he was furious. Moving up the timetable, he ordered the execution not only of those present but of the entire class of wise men throughout the city of Babylon.

This was the kind of person that Daniel was under and served for so many years. Spending time in Nebuchadnezzar's court was like playing with fire. One mistake and you get burned. Many people were still willing to do it because of the potential reward.

4. The wise men and sorcerers were unable to provide any true assistance - They failed to solve this riddle because they had no real power, authority, or divine wisdom. Much like the Egyptian magicians in the time of Moses, they played the game well. Magic, tricks, deception, and counterfeit were their tools. Their religions were false and they had no actual ability.

Exodus 8:18-19 - *The magicians tried by their secret arts to produce gnats, but they could not. So there were gnats on man and beast. Then the magicians said to Pharaoh, "This is the finger of God."*

When put up against the true miracles of God, such worldly "experts" are shown to be the frauds they are. Clever words and illusion are their game. It is a game they are good at, but it is still just a game.

This is also true of many similar people today. Speaking smoothly and cheap tricks don't denote authority, but people often fall for them.

Jesus warned us about false prophets like this who would seek to mislead even the elect if they could.

Matthew 24:24 - *For false christs and false prophets will arise and perform great signs and wonders, so as to lead astray, if possible, even the elect.*

Most cultures have people like the Babylonian wise men. For some, it is the medicine man, witch doctor, and shaman. For others, it is fortune tellers. Still more rely on religious leaders (of false religion). And in more developed countries, it is counselors holding P.H.Ds.

21

Application - Instead of turning to this kind of person who admittedly cannot solve the problem, we must turn to the One, true living God. He is the one who enables ordinary and uneducated men like Peter and John to do supernatural miracles that no earthly man can achieve.

III. Daniel wisely makes a request for time and then seeks the Lord (13-18)

Discussion Questions

- What do you notice about Daniel's response when he hears about this?
- What do you notice about his relationship with Arioch?
- How does Daniel try to find out the dream?
- Give some specific ways we can apply what we learn from Daniel here to our lives today.

Cross-References

Ecclesiastes 9:17-18 - The words of the wise heard in quiet are better than the shouting of a ruler among fools. Wisdom is better than weapons of war, but one sinner destroys much good.

Psalms 50:15 - And call upon me in the day of trouble;
I will deliver you, and you shall glorify me."

Jeremiah 33:3 - Call to me and I will answer you, and will tell you great and hidden things that you have not known.

Teaching Points

1. Daniel replied with prudence and discretion –

Throughout the whole process, we can see he was calm and careful. He was never hasty and didn't act rashly. He didn't lose his temper, panic, or get nervous. Instead, he remained cool, calm, and collected. Panicking or acting hastily is never helpful and will typically make the situation much worse.

Application – Act, don't react. Rather than rashly reacting to the situation, Daniel took the initiative to understand it and find a solution.

2. He found out more information from Arioch – The first thing that Daniel did was ask a question, "Why is the decree of the king so urgent?"

He didn't just hear part of the story and then act. He asked and then listened so that he could understand the whole picture.

Proverbs 18:13 - *If one gives an answer before he hears, it is his folly and shame.*

Application – It is vital to get all the facts about a situation before jumping in to share your opinion or solution. Many arguments could be avoided by first asking simple, neutral questions.

For example, if a husband comes home hours late, his wife might say, "You don't care about the nice meal I made. You are always late. You always put your work first." It would be much better first to ask a question, and not a loaded question such as, "Why are you home late again?"

A better question would be, "Is everything OK?" or "were you delayed?"

Neutral, fact-finding questions can help you understand the whole story rather than acting based on assumptions that may turn out to be false.

3. Daniel already had a good relationship with Arioch. His character had earned Arioch's respect over a period of time. This left him in a position to be able to help.

4. He once again asked permission for his plan - He graciously requested the king for more time (and he must have first asked Arioch to allow him an audience with the king). Daniel sought to do the will of God, but he did so under the authority God had placed over him. He was not a lone ranger going off half-cocked.

5. Daniel called in his friends to pray together with him - Once again, he was not a lone ranger. Daniel was not prideful. He wasn't using this situation to seek after his glory and get all the credit for himself. Neither did he place confidence in his powers. Instead, he surrounded himself with a team, sharing with them the details of the situation. They, in turn, could help him share the load.

And Daniel specifically asked them to "seek mercy from the God of heaven" (Daniel 2:18) so that they would not be destroyed. It was an emergency prayer meeting and Daniel wanted all hands on deck.

Application - There is strength in numbers and no matter how wise or intelligent we are, we need other believers for encouragement, counsel, and support as we seek the Lord together. When you face a difficult situation, remember that you are not alone. Go to your brothers and sisters in Christ. Share with them about your struggles. Ask them to lift up their voices with you so that together you can seek mercy from the Lord. Many times, our difficulties are compounded because we try to face them alone. God has made us part of a larger spiritual family. Let us be quick to support others and equally willing to ask for help.

6. He sought the Lord – Daniel did not only seek help from his friends. More importantly, he sought help from the Lord. No matter how wise or smart we are, if we try to do things on our own, we will fail. We must seek the Lord first because only He gives true success.

Daniel 2:19-49

Outline

I. The setting: Nebuchadnezzar's dream (1)
II. The inability and political jostling of his "wise" men (2-12)
III. Daniel wisely makes a request for time and then seeks the Lord (13-18)
IV. Daniel praises the Lord after the dream is revealed (19-23)
V. Daniel gives credit to the Lord for the interpretation (24-30)
VI. The king's dream revealed (31-35)
VII. The interpretation of the king's dream (36-45)
VIII. Daniel is rewarded (46-49)

IV. Daniel praises the Lord after the dream is revealed (19-23)

Discussion Questions

- What does Daniel do immediately after the dream is revealed to him? What can we learn from this?
- What can we learn from verse 21 about the history of the world?
- How can we know the plans of God)?

Teaching Points

1. After receiving the answer, Daniel praised God - Once the Lord revealed the answer the Daniel, he didn't just rush off and storm into the palace with it.

Reflect - What would you have probably done immediately after receiving the answer?

I probably would have been like, "thanks, Lord," and then ran off to save my life before the king decided to have me executed.

Daniel didn't do that. Once again, he was calm and realized the priority was to thank the Lord for His gracious answer to prayer truly. His response demonstrated his humility and reliance upon the Lord.

Too often, after people pray and receive the answer, they forget to thank the Lord for that answer. They are quick to ask and quick to receive but slow to express appreciation. Some take the answer for granted as if it is their right.

Application – Make time for expressing appreciation and praise to God. Instead of thinking that you have something more important to do, realize that thanking the King of Kings is the most important thing you can do.

2. Daniel recognized God's sovereign role in history –

Daniel 2:21 - *He changes times and seasons; he removes kings and sets up kings; he gives wisdom to the wise and knowledge to those who have understanding.*

God's sovereignty over history is one of the most important principles we can learn from this chapter. God is in control of the history of the world though sometimes it seems like people are. Kingdoms rise and fall. Empires grow and fade. People are born and die. But God directs everything and has a perfect plan that He will bring to completion.

We can fight with Him or against Him.

Reflect: How does recognizing God's sovereignty over the rise and fall of governments affect your attitude toward yours?

3. God the revealer –

Daniel 2:22 - *He reveals deep and hidden things; he knows what is in the darkness, and the light dwells with him.*

The only way to know the plans, thoughts, and hidden things of God, is if He reveals them to us. Contemplation, meditation, experiments, and observation, will all come back empty without going to God's revelation about Himself.

Philosophers can sit around a table and theorize, but they won't be able to understand the mind of God. A visionary can lie under a tree and meditate, but he won't be able to discover God's plans.

However, God didn't leave us in the dark. He has revealed Himself to us so that we can fully know and understand Him. While His primary revelation about Himself is through Scripture, He also reveals Himself to us through creation. In Daniel's case, it was through a vision.

Hebrews 1:1-2 - *Long ago, at many times and in many ways, God spoke to our fathers by the prophets, but in these last days he has spoken to us by his Son.*

God has used several different methods for revealing Himself to people. The good news for us is that He does.

Amos 3:7-8 - *For the Lord God does nothing without revealing his secret to his servants the prophets. The lion has roared;*
who will not fear? The Lord God has spoken; who can but prophesy?

This is a great blessing because we can know the truth and the truth will set us free.

Application – It is a great blessing that God reveals Himself to us. We should not waste that priceless opportunity to know about our Creator. Study the Word diligently so that you don't miss any part of His message to us.

V. Daniel gives credit to the Lord for the interpretation (24-30)

Discussion Questions

- What is Daniel's attitude in front of the king?
- What does he do with this opportunity?
- Give some specific ways we can follow Daniel's example in this.
- Why would God tell Nebuchadnezzar what would take place in future times?
- How did Daniel view himself in the matter?

Cross-References

Genesis 41:16 - Joseph answered Pharaoh, "It is not in me; God will give Pharaoh a favorable answer."

Acts 3:12 - And when Peter saw it he addressed the people: "Men of Israel, why do you wonder at this, or why do you stare at us, as though by our own power or piety we have made him walk?

Teaching Points

We can once again learn many things from Daniel in how he handles this situation.

1. Daniel first approaches Arioch — In every one of these interactions, Daniel follows proper procedure and recognizes established authority structures. The way he respects authority demonstrates his humility. Daniel is a prophet. God directly reveals amazing mysteries to him, but it doesn't go to Daniel's head. Again and again, Daniel works within the system to create change. He knows how to interact with high-level people.

Application: We can learn from Daniel's humility. Respect your authorities. Instead of going around them and causing them to potentially lose face, ask them for permission. At times, it may be necessary to buck the system. But don't go off half-cocked. Apply wisdom and discernment to every decision.

2. Arioch introduces Daniel —

Daniel 2:25 - *"I have found among the exiles from Judah a man who will make known to the king the interpretation."*

Arioch claims that he "found" someone who could give the interpretation to the king. This little interaction gives a glimpse into how court maneuverings worked. The way Arioch phrased this introduction seems designed to get credit for himself and curry favor with Nebuchadnezzar.

Most of the officials in the court would have done likewise. There was constant jockeying as each person attempted to attract the spotlight. The way Daniel interacts with the king is a night-and-day difference.

3. Daniel is bold and confident - He doesn't cringe, fret, or worry. The way he interacts with the king exudes confidence. But it is not confidence in himself. He has the answer from the Lord, who is on his side. He has nothing to worry about and no reason to fear.

Romans 8:31 - *What then shall we say to these things? If God is for us, who can be against us?*

4. He gives credit to the Lord -

Daniel 2:27-28 - *Daniel answered the king and said, "No wise men, enchanters, magicians, or astrologers can show to the king the mystery that the king has asked, but there is a God in heaven who reveals mysteries, and he has made known to King Nebuchadnezzar what will be in the latter days.*

Here was a prime opportunity for Daniel to gain recognition and increase his standing in Babylon. None of the other wise men of the city would have hesitated to toot their own horns. They would have milked the moment for everything it was worth trying to increase their reward. However, Daniel sees this not as an opportunity for self-aggrandization but for glorifying God on a very public stage.

The Lord had given Daniel a great gift, but like Joseph before him, Daniel used his gift for God and not for personal gain. He gives all the honor and glory to God. He uses the chance to preach about the true God and exalt Him.

He had his moment in the sun and he didn't use it selfishly. Instead, he seized the chance to share the truth about God. He was using his gift and his position for the Lord.

Application: Seek every chance to glorify God. Sometimes, people praise you for certain gifts or abilities you possess. Other times, you will have a unique platform for testifying of God. Don't let those opportunities go to waste. Be bold and shine the light of Christ.

5. He remained humble –

Daniel 2:30 - *But as for me, this mystery has been revealed to me, not because of any wisdom that I have more than all the living, but in order that the interpretation may be made known to the king, and that you may know the thoughts of your mind.*

He recognized it was not through any talent or wisdom of his own. He was only a tool to accomplish God's purposes.

VI. The king's dream revealed (31-35)

Discussion Questions

- This same prophecy is repeated in chapter 7 when the various kingdoms are beasts. Why the difference?
- Does God normally speak in dreams today? Why or why not?
- How does he speak to us?

Cross-References

Hebrews 1:1-2 - Long ago, at many times and in many ways, God spoke to our fathers by the prophets, but in these last days he has spoken to us by his Son.

Teaching Points

1. The layered statute – Nebuchadnezzar saw a "great image." It was "mighty" and "bright" with a "frightening" appearance. It had a head of gold, chest and arms of silver, middle and thighs of bronze, legs of iron, and feet of iron and clay. A stone then comes and strikes the feet of the statue. The statue was shattered and scattered without a trace, leaving only the stone remaining. And the stone grew and filled the earth like a giant mountain.

Without God's special revelation, the interpretation of this dream would not be possible!

VII. The interpretation of the king's dream (36-45)

Discussion Questions

- Did this dream come true?
- Which parts of this dream have not yet been fulfilled?
- What would you say is the main point of the dream?
- When is this final kingdom going to be established?

- What do you think the term "without hands" signifies?

Teaching Points

1. Interpretation of the dream – Nebuchadnezzar's Babylon was the head of gold. Daniel states this clearly in verse 38. After that, each section of the statue represents one kingdom. Bible scholars agree that the silver chest and arms represent Medo-Persia, the middle and thighs of bronze represent Greece, and the legs of iron represent Rome. Most also agree that the feet of iron and clay represent a still-future-to-us kingdom. That kingdom will be the revived Roman empire and rise to power in the end times.

Meanwhile, the rock made without hands represents a kingdom that God will set up. It will be the final kingdom. Never will that kingdom be destroyed, but He will reign forever.

2 World kingdoms look powerful and wealthy but will fade –

Gold, silver, and bronze are all shiny and attractive. These are valuable metals. And even in the dream, they were bright and inviting. Iron is known for its strength. From man's standpoint, the world empires and kingdoms are incredible, rich, strong, and magnificent.

Reflect: What comparisons do you think there might be between the specific metals for each kingdom and the qualities of that kingdom?

But all of the kingdoms of the world are temporary. They will rise and fall. Each will be conquered and taken over by another. Finally, they will be scattered without a trace. Nothing will remain of these world powers. They are a visible testament to the fleeting nature of riches and power.

Their passing reminds us that the world and all that it offers are fading. Many people put their trust in governments. Some serve these governments out of conviction. More serve out of the desire for reward and power. All of those who link their futures and livelihood to the world will be disappointed. Just as Babylon the Great will fall in the end-times (Revelation 18), so will all kingdoms of the world.

1 John 2:15-17 - *Do not love the world or the things in the world. If anyone loves the world, the love of the Father is not in him. For all that is in the world—the desires of the flesh and the desires of the eyes and pride of life—is not from the Father but is from the*

31

world. And the world is passing away along with its desires, but whoever does the will of God abides forever.

Application: Does the world look shiny and attractive to you? Are you pursuing the world for what it can offer you? Remember the words of Jesus, "Heaven and earth will pass away, but my words shall endure forever." (Luke 21:33.)

Let's say you are going to invest in the stock market. You are choosing between two companies. And you have critical information. One of these companies will go bankrupt and close its doors in ten years. The other company will continually increase its market share and become the most successful company the world has ever seen. Where are you going to invest your money? It's an easy decision, right?

Likewise, build your treasure in heaven and not on earth.

2. The toes of the feet depict the ten kingdoms that will make up the end-times kingdom – That future kingdom is described throughout the book of Revelation. The antichrist will be its head. It will be an utterly wicked and blasphemous alliance of nations where Satan worship will be promoted. And all those who refuse to show their loyalty by receiving the mark of the beast will be martyred.

Since the legs of iron represent Rome and the toes have iron and clay, most scholars agree this will be a revived Roman Empire rising from the civilizations left behind after the collapse of Rome.

3. The final and everlasting kingdom - This kingdom will be made "without hands," a symbol of its divine origin. It will be an eternal and lasting kingdom. All other civilizations made use of the structures and peoples left behind when they were conquered and were in turn, left for others. But not this one.

It will strike the feet of iron and clay. This end-times kingdom will set itself up in direct opposition to the Lord and everything good He stands for. Satan's puppet, the antichrist himself, will be at its head. Promises of riches, peace, prosperity, utopia, and complete freedom to engage in sin of every kind will be used to lure people into its chains of bondage. The alliance of nations will go so far as to gather the world's armies together to challenge the Lord of Hosts. They will gather at Armageddon to try to end God once and for all (Revelation 16-20).

Then Jesus will return. The rock will shatter this kingdom and its armies. And Jesus will set up a kingdom that will have no end.

4. It is an exciting period to live in - A journey of thousands of years is winding down towards a destination that might be around the next bend! Many things are happening which appear to be setting the stage for the end-times events in Daniel and Revelation to be fulfilled. We don't know the day of Jesus' return, but at no time in world history before now has it been so close at hand.

VIII. Daniel is rewarded (46-49)

Teaching Points

1. Nebuchadnezzar fell on his face and paid homage to Daniel – Can you imagine that? The most powerful man in the world bowed to a teenager, an exile from Judah! He then gave glory to God.

Daniel 2:47 - *The king answered and said to Daniel, "Truly, your God is God of gods and Lord of kings, and a revealer of mysteries, for you have been able to reveal this mystery."*

Nebuchadnezzar still is not a genuine believer (see Daniel 3), but it is clear that God is doing work in his heart.

2. Daniel didn't seek a reward, but he received it –

1 Peter 5:6 - *Humble yourselves, therefore, under the mighty hand of God so that at the proper time he may exalt you.*

This verse was fulfilled in Daniel. Although Daniel didn't seek personal recognition, wealth, or power, he got them because he was faithful to the Lord. Just as with Solomon, God often gives these things as a bonus to those not seeking them.

3. Daniel asked for his friends' promotion – Daniel was wise and bold. While he made no requests for himself, he took advantage of this golden

opportunity to bring his friends' names to the king. Even during this time of triumph, Daniel did not forget his friends.

He demonstrated a fundamental Biblical principle, which is to ask.

Matthew 7:7 - *Ask, and it will be given to you; seek, and you will find; knock, and it will be opened to you.*

Often we don't have because we don't' ask. Sometimes fear can prevent us from speaking up and making a request. However, not making the request virtually guarantees it won't be granted!

Application: What can you learn from this week's lesson to apply to your life this week?

Daniel 3

Outline

I. All the people were to worship Nebuchadnezzar's image under threat of death (1-7)
II. The accusation against the Jews (8-12)
III. Nebuchadnezzar furiously threatens their life and defies the Lord (13-15)
IV. The three friends trust in the Lord and refuse to give in (16-18)
V. Nebuchadnezzar is enraged (19-23)
VI. The Lord protects them from the fire (24-27)
VII. Nebuchadnezzar acknowledges the Lord and blesses the three men (28-30)

I. All the people were to worship Nebuchadnezzar's image under threat of death (1-7)

Discussion Questions

- What were the dimensions of this image?
- What kind of image do you think it was?
- Why did Nebuchadnezzar want the people to worship this image?
- Who was invited?
- Do you think all the people worshiping that image at that moment truly believed in it?
- So why would they worship it?
- What do you think most people would do today in the same situation?
- What does this show us about men's hearts?

Cross-References

Isaiah 40:19-20 - An idol! A craftsman casts it, and a goldsmith overlays it with gold and casts for it silver chains. He who is too impoverished for an offering chooses wood that will not rot; he seeks out a skillful craftsman to set up an idol that will not move.

Matthew 4:9 - And he said to him, "All these I will give you, if you will fall down and worship me."

Teaching Points

1. Nebuchadnezzar made an image of gold – Chapter 2 finished with the king giving glory to God and saying that Daniel's God is "God of gods and Lord of kings." However, that newfound humility proved to be short-lived.

The dream was intended to convey a message that God is sovereign over all kings. While the kingdoms of this world are temporary and will finally be destroyed, His kingdom is eternal. Though Nebuchadnezzar was represented by the head of gold, the entire statue was shattered by the Lord.

Instead of learning humility and submitting himself to the "God of gods," the Babylonian king went the other way. He seemingly became even more egotistical, if that was possible. Nebuchadnezzar built an entire statue dedicated to himself. Just being the head wasn't enough. He wanted the whole thing! Note that the figure was made out of gold. It was almost as if he was saying, "The head is not enough. I am not just the head. I am everything!"

The image was 90 feet (27.4 meters) tall and 9 feet (2.7 meters) wide. Though the proportions are too narrow for an average human figure, these measurements could include an elevated base with a human figure perched on top.

The size of the hulking image was meant to impress and intimidate. It was almost as tall as the Colossus of Rhodes.

Nebuchadnezzar's "repentance" didn't last long. Often people's immediate response to an exciting spiritual experience is to become pious. But piety that is based on an emotional or dramatic event generally doesn't last. When life gets back to normal, it is easy to fall right back into old habits.

Application – You may be able to think back on your life and remember an event (perhaps a trial or a victory) that made you feel excited and close to God. Perhaps you made a resolution to surrender some aspect of your life to the Lord. But as time passed and things got back to normal, you slipped into old habits. What are some causes of that? How can you be better rooted so that your life isn't typified by "one step forward, one step back?"

2. Nebuchadnezzar required all the officials in the kingdom to worship the image - It was a vast kingdom spread across a diverse population. That diversity could cause issues or potential rebellion. Politically, one religion could unify the empire.

Once again, it shows us that Nebuchadnezzar was a clever ruler.

4. It satisfied Nebuchadnezzar's pride – Likely, this was not just a calculated attempt to unify the kingdom but was primarily to massage Nebuchadnezzar's ego. He loved the power. He enjoyed exerting his control over others by forcing them to bow to his every whim.

Like many rulers, his power made him increasingly prideful to the point where he craved worship.

5. The culture was quite advanced and featured choirs/bands.

6. Music has a powerful effect, either for good or evil. Satan often uses music to his own ends.

7. The people were like sheep – It seems that every single official gathered from the entire realm succumbed and worshiped the image, except Daniel's friends.

Reflect: Why did these people worship the image? Did they believe in this religion that Babylon was selling?

They worshiped because it was to their material advantage to do so, not because they believed. Likely, most of those gathered didn't have any genuine faith in this newly constructed statue. For many, it represented a god that was foreign to them.

Yet they didn't have the backbone to stand up for their beliefs, whatever they were. It shows the weakness of most people and their principles. Most people have a price. Offer them enough and their principles go out the window.

In this case, the price was their life. People are all about pragmatism. Feigning respect for this idol was a small price, they thought, compared to their lives.

Matthew 16:26 - *For what will it profit a man if he gains the whole world and forfeits his soul? Or what shall a man give in return for his soul?*

What they didn't realize is that their souls are infinitely more important than their physical lives.

Many professing believers in Christ approach their faith with this same pragmatic bent. They think God will give them many material blessings or grant them perfect health. But when they face trials or other difficulties, they abandon their faith.

Once when I was sharing the gospel, a person asked me, "if I believe in Jesus, what do I get?" While it is not often voiced so plainly, this attitude often lurks behind the surface.

II. The accusation against the Jews (8-12)

Discussion Questions

- Why do you think the Chaldeans tattle-tailed?
- Why did they refuse to bow?
- What reasons/justifications could they have given for bowing?
- Can you think of similar examples today where "everyone" is doing something wrong?
- What kind of temptations have you faced where the vast majority of your peers were all engaging in the wrong behavior?
- What kind of reasons do we sometimes give for why we "have" to do the same as everyone else?
- What will happen if we don't?
- What should we do? Why?

Cross-References

Proverbs 27:4 - Wrath is cruel, anger is overwhelming, but who can stand before jealousy?

Teaching Points

1. Certain Chaldeans maliciously accused the Jews – One gets the sense that these court officials were constantly jockeying for position. While they must have appeared very polite and well-mannered on the outside, they were ready to stab you in the back and take your job at the slightest opportunity.

Undoubtedly, Daniel and his friends' success was a sore point for these officials. The Jews were foreigners taking jobs that should have rightfully been theirs! Their attacks were not motivated by genuine loyalty to the king but by jealousy.

Daniel 3:12 - *These men, O king, pay no attention to you; they do not serve your gods or worship the golden image that you have set up.*

The accusation itself was made as harshly as possible. They said that these men "pay no attention to you." It is as if they want to incite the king's anger against them. At the same time, their wording makes it sound as if they are simply concerned for Nebuchadnezzar's well-being.

In reality, their hope was the Jews would be punished and if some of them were promoted to take the vacancy, even better!

1 Peter 3:16-17 - *Having a good conscience, so that, when you are slandered, those who revile your good behavior in Christ may be put to shame. For it is better to suffer for doing good, if that should be God's will, than for doing evil.*

Daniel's friends faced malicious attacks. They were treated as criminals. But for believers, it is a badge of honor to suffer for the Lord. As Peter said, it is "better to suffer for doing good than for doing evil."

Application – When we face difficulties or suffering, we should examine ourselves to see if our own behavior has caused it. If your sin caused the negative consequences, don't blame others or say, "it is my cross to bear." Instead, repent of your sin. But if it is persecution due to standing up for

Christ, then stand firm.

3. The Jews were the only ones (mentioned) that didn't bow and worship the image —

Imagine the enormous pressure they would have faced. Already, they were isolated far from their home country. Removed from their support group, they were thrust into the middle of this high-pressure situation. All around them on every side, thousands of people prostrated themselves in accordance with the king's command.

How conspicuous it must have been for the three of them to remain standing. There was no way to hide, nowhere to run, and no possibility of even disguising their disobedience.

And yet they stood firm. These were men of conviction. They knew the Old Testament prohibitions against worshiping or bowing to an idol.

Exodus 20:4-5 - *You shall not make for yourself a carved image, or any likeness of anything that is in heaven above, or that is in the earth beneath, or that is in the water under the earth. You shall not bow down to them or serve them, for I the Lord your God am a jealous God.*

For them, it was a straightforward choice. Bowing down to the idol would have been disobedience to God. Therefore they chose to obey God rather than man. It wasn't a decision that was made blindly. They were wise men and would have known that the likely penalty was death. Obedience to God was prioritized over their own lives and they were willing to face the cost, whatever it was.

Such faithfulness is rare but refreshing.

Reflect – Are you willing to risk your life in obedience to God?

Application – We don't face "life or death" faith choices very often. And it can be difficult to know exactly how we would respond. What we do face is hundreds of "small" tests every day to obey God or pursue self. Jesus said that "he who is faithful in a little thing is also faithful in much." The best training ground to prepare for moments of intense persecution is the daily grind. Practice obedience on a daily basis and this will strengthen your walk with the Lord and prepare you for challenging tests.

4. The three friends did not justify compromise – They could have offered various excuses for giving in. Or they could have come up with some other plan.

Reflect – Would it have been acceptable for them to take a "sick day?" How about choosing the moment when everyone was bowing to pick up a pebble, clean their sandal, or draw in the dirt?

Bowing down (even if they didn't truly worship the idol in their heart) would have caused them to lose their testimony. By doing that, they would have been the same as the other court officials, sacrificing principles for personal gain.

5. Satan often uses threats or rewards to lure believers into sin -

Reflect – Share a time when you were threatened (or offered a reward) to entice you to sin.

He also tries to get us to compromise and worship false things because what you worship is what you will become like.

5. "Everyone is doing it" and "I have no choice" are justifications as old as time –

It is tough to stand against a current that is moving in one direction. The winds of culture and public opinion are powerful forces. The last few years have shown that when an idea starts to become "trendy" or "cool," people quickly pile on the bandwagon. Social norms and traditions can change almost overnight. What is considered shameful one day is praised as virtuous soon after.

When the tidal forces of media and public opinion start flowing, it may feel that there is nothing you can do. It may feel like you don't have a choice.

Yet this account of Hananiah, Mishael, and Azariah reminds us that we always have a choice. Compromise is never mandatory. God has given you a will. You can form your own convictions from God's Word. And you can then stand on those convictions even in the face of enormous pressure.

When you stand before God one day, He will not accept "everyone was doing it" as a legitimate reason for why you were doing it.

Romans 14:4 - *Who are you to pass judgment on the servant of another? It is before his own master that he stands or falls. And he will be upheld, for the Lord is able to make him stand.*

Each of us will stand before the Lord one day. And the Lord wants you to pass the judgment that day. So we need to stand now. It is not by our own power that we can overcome. It is only through Christ. The Lord gives strength.

Revelation 12:11 - *And they have conquered him by the blood of the Lamb and by the word of their testimony, for they loved not their lives even unto death.*

Application – Do not give in to pressure. The world seeks to mold you to its image, but God wants to conform you to His image. Stand firm on the side of righteousness, even if you are the only person in your family, class, company, or the world to do so.

III. Nebuchadnezzar furiously threatens their life and defies the Lord (13-15)

Discussion Questions

- How did Nebuchadnezzar feel about the situation?
- Was he ready to forgive them?
- Did he have any genuine belief in any gods?
- Did he respect the God of the Jews?
- What often happens when someone defies God? Examples? (Goliath, Titanic Belshazzar, etc.)

Cross-References

Esther 3:5 - And when Haman saw that Mordecai did not bow down or pay homage to him, Haman was filled with fury.

Exodus 5:2 - But Pharaoh said, "Who is the Lord, that I should obey his voice and let Israel go? I do not know the Lord, and moreover, I will not let Israel go."

2 Kings 18:35 - Who among all the gods of the lands have delivered their lands out of my hand, that the Lord should deliver Jerusalem out of my hand?

Teaching Points

1. When Nebuchadnezzar heard that three people had refused to obey his orders, he was furious –

The king was used to blind obedience. Few people would have dared to question him. Fewer still would have defied him. It was simply unheard of to disobey. Based on his reaction, it seems that Nebuchadnezzar could not believe it. And he could not handle it.

Didn't they know that he had the power to have them killed? Didn't they know that he held their lives in his hands? He is the head of gold! The most splendid king the world had ever seen! And here they were, three Jewish boys with the gall to refuse a direct order. They must not have understood. Yes, that's it. There was a miscommunication somewhere along the way.

2. He was willing to give them another chance –

Was Nebuchadnezzar showing his soft, compassionate side? More likely, he offered them another opportunity in order to save his own face. It didn't look good for Nebuchadnezzar the Great to be defied this way in public. He had to take control of the situation and show his empire who was in charge. And he had to prove to himself that he could force anyone to do anything he wanted. After all, he was the head of gold! Not the feet, the head!

3. He defied their God –

Daniel 3:15 - *And who is the god who will deliver you out of my hands?*

The king is not the only one who made threats like this. Many other characters in Scripture did the same. Spoiler: it doesn't usually end well for those who defy God.

IV. The three friends trust in the Lord and refuse to give in (16-18)

Discussion Questions

- Did the Jews consider giving in? Why not?
- What enabled them to stand firm, even in the face of faith?
- Were they willing to give their lives for it, or did they just expect God to save them?
- What should this teach us about the motivation to do right?

Cross-References

Matthew 10:19-20 - When they deliver you over, do not be anxious how you are to speak or what you are to say, for what you are to say will be given to you in that hour. For it is not you who speak, but the Spirit of your Father speaking through you.

Psalms 27:1-2 - The LORD is my light and my salvation; whom shall I fear? The LORD is the stronghold of my life; of whom shall I be afraid? When evildoers assail me to eat up my flesh, my adversaries and foes, it is they who stumble and fall.

Isaiah 12:2 - Behold, God is my salvation; I will trust, and will not be afraid; for the Lord God is my strength and my song, and he has become my salvation.

Luke 1:37 - For nothing will be impossible with God.

Teaching Points

Daniel 3:16-18 - *Shadrach, Meshach, and Abednego answered and said to the king, "O Nebuchadnezzar, we have no need to answer you in this matter. If this be so, our God whom we serve is able to deliver us from the burning fiery furnace, and he will deliver us out of your hand, O king. But if not, be it known to you, O king, that we will not serve your gods or worship the golden image that you have set up."*

This is one of the most remarkable declarations of faith you will ever see.

1. Shadrach, Meshach, and Abednego's declaration of faith –

They didn't even consider giving in. It was never an option. Their determination was clearly conveyed to the king. Like Daniel in chapter 1, the communication was clear and respectful. There isn't a hint of rudeness or arrogance. Nonetheless, their resolve was firm.

Application - When the battle lines are drawn, it is essential to declare your position. The longer you allow a temptation to linger in your mind without taking decisive action, the more likely you will succumb to it.

Have the correct principles and make up your mind ahead of time to stand firm. Don't negotiate. There is no negotiation on God's clear commands. Once you start negotiating, you've already lost the battle (Eve).

2. We have no need to answer you - Shadrach, Meshach, and Abednego were accountable to God. They clearly understood that God was the judge. He is the one on the throne. And He is the one to whom they answered. Although Nebuchadnezzar thought that he was the supreme ruler over all, there was One still higher still.

Application – Understand that each of us is ultimately accountable to God. Many people may seek to set themselves up as the authority over us. And God does establish authority structures. The problem is when people make themselves out to be the ultimate authority, whether that is a government, a boss, or even parents seeking to control grown children. Remembering that God is the one you need to answer to simplifies our decisions and crystalizes what is important.

3. We will not serve your gods or worship the golden image you have set up –

Like Daniel in chapter 1, the three friends decided they were not going to cross this line. It wasn't a negotiation. Threats to their life would make no difference. Their determination was firm.

Seeing the clarity of their thoughts and speed of reply, they likely discussed their response to the image before the day of the dedication even arrived. Their minds were already made up.

These young men had counted the costs and there was no turning back.

Application – It is critical to resolve in your mind not to compromise before you ever face a potentially compromising situation. For example, sex before marriage should be a red line for believers. Don't wait to make that decision in the heat of the moment. You should make this commitment before God long before you ever face that moment of opportunity/temptation.

4. They were willing to give their lives for it - They knew God could save them, but even if He didn't, they would still stand firm in the faith. They weren't like all of the others, merely pragmatically motivated. It wasn't about what they could get. It was about what was right.

Some professing believers are willing to obey God as long as God blesses them and rewards them. But when trouble comes, they just give up. It's not worth it to them. Let us follow the example of these three faithful men by committing ourselves to stand firm on the rock even if it costs us something (or everything).

5. Their faith was deep - They had a rock-solid faith in the Lord and in His power, knowing He was in control.

Acknowledging before God that the people around us who exercise authority are themselves under His is half the battle.

Our teachers, parents, boss, and friends may seem powerful now, but they won't once we face the Lord. Our primary responsibility is to serve the Lord, not men.

6. What is humility – Daniel's friends were humble. They did not think overly highly of themselves or their own lives. Rather, they realized that God may or may not save them. These three young men saw themselves as God did. While they were valuable in His sight, their lives were less important than God's divine plan.

Humility is not equal to weakness or groveling. The band spoke boldly and clearly. Having a backbone, the trio stood up straight and refused to bow.

Many think that believers are weak or timid. We see that is not the case. Boldness and humility are complementary, not mutually exclusive. Knowing that your life is in God's hands and He is completely sovereign (humility) gives boldness.

V. Nebuchadnezzar is enraged (19-23)

Discussion Questions

- Did Nebuchadnezzar respect their decision?
- Do you think people in the world will respect our decision if we stand up for what is right?
- How would you describe Nebuchadnezzar and his attitude here?

Teaching Points

1. Nebuchadnezzar was filled with fury and the expression of his face changed –

The mighty ruler thought that he exercised total control over all of his subjects. Finding out that they had minds and a will of their own, enraged him. Nebuchadnezzar was so angry that he almost popped a vein.

Here is a man who was used to absolute power. Most likely, no one had ever defied him before. Throughout the events of the book of Daniel, we see that God wanted to teach Nebuchadnezzar a healthy dose of humility.

2. He ordered the furnace heated seven times more –

The trio was about to discover it wasn't a false threat.

Wisdom can sometimes help God's people avoid this type of showdown. For example, Daniel's wisdom helped him find another solution to the pagan food problem.

But sometimes, these things cannot be worked out. Sometimes there is no recourse but to boldly take a stand and let the chips fall where they may.

2. Nebuchadnezzar caused the death of the people who were serving him.

Daniel 3:22 - *Because the king's order was urgent and the furnace overheated, the flame of the fire killed those men who took up Shadrach, Meshach, and Abednego.*

Foolish decisions are always harmful. But they cause even more harm when those in authority make them because their poor choices negatively affect many under them.

Application – Don't make decisions in haste that will hurt those under you (children, employees, students, etc.) If you are angry, it is better to cool off before making a decision. Decisions made in anger often cause regret.

VI. The Lord protects them from the fire (24-27)

Discussion Questions

- Who do you think was walking around in the fire with them?
- Why?
- How complete was the miracle?

Cross-References

Hebrews 11:34 - Quenched the power of fire, escaped the edge of the sword, were made strong out of weakness, became mighty in war, put foreign armies to flight.

Teaching Points

Daniel 3:24-25 - *Then King Nebuchadnezzar was astonished and rose up in haste. He declared to his counselors, "Did we not cast three men bound into the fire?" They answered and said to the king, "True, O king." He answered and said, "But I see four men unbound, walking in the midst of the fire, and they are not hurt; and the appearance of the fourth is like a son of the gods."*

1. The Lord Himself was with them in the flames –

A fourth person was seen walking around amid the fire. This could have been an angel, but more likely was Jesus pre-incarnate.

Isaiah 43:2 - *When you pass through the waters, I will be with you; and through the rivers, they shall not overwhelm you; when you walk through fire you shall not be burned, and the flame shall not consume you.*

God did not abandon His faithful followers. Neither did He allow them to succumb to the pain or death of the fire.

When we have faith in God, He will honor that. Regardless of what we face, He will be with us in the midst of it.

The three friends rightly said that God might not save them. He doesn't promise to save us from every trouble. The account of Shadrach, Meshach, and Abednego is also not a promise that God will always deliver us out of trials.

Many believers have been martyred. Many prophets in the Old Testament were persecuted or killed because of their message. God's Son Himself was not saved but was delivered to death.

What God does promise is that He will do according to what is best in each situation (Romans 8:28).

Another promise is that He will be with us and never abandon us.

Hebrews 13:5 - *Keep your life free from love of money, and be content with what you have, for he has said, "I will never leave you nor forsake you."*

Reflect – How does God show His comforting presence to believers in the midst of trials? How have you personally experienced that?

2. Those who defy God are setting themselves up for defeat –

Pride goes before the fall.

James 4:6 - *But he gives more grace. Therefore it says, "God opposes the proud but gives grace to the humble."*

3. God's miracles are not done halfway - There could be no doubt about the miraculous nature of this event because of the evidence of the clothes, hair, and rope. No part of them or their clothing gave any indication that they had been even near a fire.

And let us not forget that the soldiers who threw them in (and clearly would have tried to stay as far from the fire as possible) were themselves killed by the extreme heat.

The fire burned the ropes binding them and didn't touch the rest. God's miracles leave no room for coincidences. He wanted everyone who saw this miracle to clearly know that He was behind it. They got the message.

VII. Nebuchadnezzar acknowledges the Lord and blesses the three men (28-30)

Discussion Questions

- Is this the point where Nebuchadnezzar becomes a believer?
- Does he respect their decision now?
- Do you think God will save us as well?
  How did God use this event in the kingdom of Babylon?
- How about in the lives of the three Jews?
- What do you think they learned from this event?

Cross-References

Psalms 33:18-19 - Behold, the eye of the LORD is on those who fear him, on those who hope in his steadfast love, that he may deliver their soul from death and keep them alive in famine.

Psalms 34:22 - The LORD redeems the life of his servants; none of those who take refuge in him will be condemned.

Teaching Points

1. Nebuchadnezzar acknowledged the Lord to some extent –

Although he acknowledged God, he only recognized the Lord as one impressive God among many gods. He wasn't repentant and his story is not yet over.

2. God had a plan for the whole kingdom –

The decision of the three to stand up for their faith made life easier for the rest of the believers scattered across the kingdom. A decree was given that prohibited anyone from even speaking against their God.

Their obedience turned an evil day that looked like defeat for God's followers into an amazing testimony. All over the kingdom, people heard this incredible story of God's power. And it wasn't only spread through word of mouth, but also through official decree direct from the throne!

If the three exiles had compromised like everyone else, the result would have been a terrible lost opportunity for building God's kingdom.

Our right decisions can help others. Sometimes it just takes one person standing up for truth to bring exposure to bad policies, shame to evil practices, and be a catalyst for change. If everyone goes with the status quo, nothing will change. But through the faithful, God can bring change. Stories of God's people standing up for what is right can spread the faith, inspire millions worldwide, and ultimately bring glory to God.

3. Shadrach, Meshach, and Abednego were promoted! –

What once again looked like not only a career killer but a life killer ended up being a career booster. The faithful trio prospered more than ever before and were set above many of those who bowed down to this idol. Nebuchadnezzar may have thought he had ultimate power, but God was holding the strings!

Application – Spend some time in reflection. Choose one area where you feel pressure that is hard for you to take a stand. Ask God to show you what you need to do. Pray for strength. And resolve to stand firm.

Daniel 4

Outline

I. Nebuchadnezzar addresses the nation with praise for God (1-3)
II. Nebuchadnezzar has another dream: only Daniel can interpret it (4-8)
III. Nebuchadnezzar relates the dream (9-18)
IV. Daniel interprets the dream (19-27)
V. The dream is fulfilled (28-33)
VI. Nebuchadnezzar repents, is restored, and praises God (34-37)

I. Nebuchadnezzar addresses the nation with praise for God (1-3)

Discussion Questions

- Why do you think Nebuchadnezzar wanted to declare the things God had done?
- Why would he be willing to bring public shame on himself for the embarrassing episode?
- If something like this happens to you, would you like to share it with everyone?
- What does the fact that he was willing to share it show about his new attitude?

Cross-references

Psalms 92:1-2 - It is good to give thanks to the LORD, to sing praises to your name, O Most High; to declare your steadfast love in the morning, and your faithfulness by night.

Psalms 66:16 - Come and hear, all you who fear God, and I will tell what he has done for my soul.

Psalms 72:18 - Blessed be the LORD, the God of Israel, who alone does wondrous things.

Psalms 86:10 - For you are great and do wondrous things; you alone are God.

Teaching Points

1. Nebuchadnezzar praises God – This chapter is like a movie that shows a shocking ending, backs up, and shows how the story arrived at that surprising conclusion.

The king makes a surprising declaration to the nation. In his proclamation, he praises the "Most High God." He gives the Lord glory while finally admitting that God's kingdom is "an everlasting kingdom."

Throughout the first three chapters of Daniel, we have seen God working in the king's life to teach him humility. In chapter 2, God sends a vision to Nebuchadnezzar of the statue. The purpose of that vision was to remind him that even the most powerful human civilizations would fall, but God's kingdom would endure forever. Instead of responding with humility and submitting himself to God, Nebuchadnezzar built an idol (reminiscent of the golden head) and demanded everyone in his empire worship it. The vision went to his head!

God, therefore, used the occasion of the dedication of the image to remind Nebuchadnezzar of who was really on the throne. The Lord crashed the party. His three chosen instruments would not bow down to the idol. The king was furious and had them thrown into the furnace. He thought his power was absolute. But God protected their lives and once again demonstrated that He was the King of Kings.

After this, Nebuchadnezzar made a perfunctory statement about God's greatness. But it was just a temporary blip, and soon he reverted to his arrogant ways.

And then, boom, out of nowhere comes this seemingly very sincere and heartfelt proclamation of praise to God. Where did this come from? Why the change of heart?

God must have done something truly extraordinary to humble Nebuchadnezzar. And that is the story he shares with the nation here. He humbles himself to share a testimony, even when that story highlights the depth of his own sin and shame.

Application – Throughout the course of our lives, God will teach us many lessons. Some of those lessons are painful. Sometimes we are brought low and dragged through the gutter (many times because of our own choices). In each of those events, God is working. Rather than hide our sins and project an image of perfection, we should be vulnerable. Open up and testify of God's grace in your lives. Our goal should not be to look good but to exalt God. What testimony of God's goodness can you share?

II. Nebuchadnezzar has another dream: only Daniel can interpret it (4-8)

Discussion Questions

- What similarities are there between this and the last time Nebuchadnezzar had a dream?
- Why do you think he would turn to the ineffective "wise" men again?
- Did he believe Daniel could solve this problem? Why didn't he turn to Daniel sooner?
- Can you think of any comparable situations in the world where people keep turning to something ineffective? (Turn to politicians)
- Why do they do it?
- Why do people not want to turn to God/Church/Believers more?

Cross-References

Luke 12:19-20 - And I will say to my soul, "Soul, you have ample goods laid up for many years; relax, eat, drink, be merry.'" But God said to him, Fool! This night your soul is required of you, and the things you have prepared, whose will they be?'

Isaiah 44:24-26 - Thus says the Lord, your Redeemer, who formed you from the womb: "I am the Lord, who made all things, who alone stretched out the heavens, who spread out the earth by myself, who frustrates the signs of liars and makes fools of diviners, who turns wise men back and makes their knowledge foolish, who confirms the word of his servant and fulfills the counsel of his messengers."

Teaching Points

1. I was at ease in my house and prospering in my palace – Nebuchadnezzar had an easy life. He was rich and powerful. Servants stood by 24-7 answering his beck and call. What did the king do with his power and prosperity?

There is no evidence that Nebuchadnezzar sought to reach out and help others. Instead of using the resources God had given him to improve the lives of his subjects, Nebuchadnezzar lived a very self-absorbed life. His focus was on his own pleasure, power, and prosperity. With thoughts centered on himself, Nebuchadnezzar was the object of his own most profound admiration.

2. I saw a dream that made me afraid – It is the second time God communicated with the pagan despot through a dream. Notice when he had this dream. It was when everything was going smoothly and he was enjoying the good life in the palace.

He wasn't seeking God, but God was seeking Him. God took the initiative to reach out and communicate with Nebuchadnezzar when he was enjoying his merry life.

From this, we can learn two lessons.

A. Don't get too comfortable! Pride goes before the fall. Live humbly in complete reliance upon God daily, not just when things are going poorly.

Micah 6:8 - *He has told you, O man, what is good; and what does the Lord require of you but to do justice, and to love kindness, and to walk humbly with your God?*

If we don't keep our focus on God, then don't be surprised if He intervenes in our lives to turn our attention back to its rightful place.

B. God is the one who takes the initiative in our relationship with Him. We love because He first loved us. This is one aspect of His character which we should appreciate. It reminds us that our salvation is not due to our own goodness but to His mercy. And if He sought us out while we were still sinners (Romans 5:8), how much more is it true that He will remain faithful when we are already saved?

3. I made a decree that all the wise men should be brought before me –

Whenever Nebuchadnezzar faced a complicated puzzle, he called in the empire's experts. It was an esteemed group that included wise men, magicians, enchanters, Chaldeans, and astrologers. Each group was a special class specifically trained to aid the king in these challenging matters.

How they managed to hold on to their jobs all this time beats me! Once again, they failed to solve their potentate's problem. The only thing they seem to be good at is consistency. They are consistently totally inept in understanding or communicating the things of God.

While they were experts at the magic and sorcery the Babylonian religion was based on, they didn't know the true God and were therefore of no help in understanding Him or His message. Though they looked and sounded clever, they were blind leaders of the blind.

Reflect - Why did Nebuchadnezzar keep calling for help from these wise men?

Application – Go to the right people for counsel and help. If you need help with a math problem, go to a math teacher. If you need help with a medical issue, go to a doctor. If you need help with a moral or spiritual problem, go to a godly believer.

4. At last, Daniel came in before me – Daniel should have been plan A but somehow was still plan Z. The fact that Daniel came in last seems to indicate that Nebuchadnezzar was still reluctant to embrace Daniel's God. It was as if the king was hoping that his own native gods would come through. When they didn't (as he may have expected all along), he had no choice but to turn to Daniel if he wanted the answer.

In verse 8, Nebuchadnezzar emphasized that Daniel's name was Belteshazzar, "after the name of my god." He is writing this after his life-changing experience. And the way he emphasizes this fact (and the fact that Daniel came in last) contrasts the true power of Yahweh with his weak gods.

III. Nebuchadnezzar relates the dream (9-18)

Discussion Questions

- What is an angelic watcher?
- What role did he have?
- How long do you think is seven periods of time?

Cross-References

Teaching Points

1. I know that the spirit of the holy gods is in you – Nebuchadnezzar had already witnessed amazing miracles in the lives of Daniel and his friends. God had been working in his life through them. There was clearly something different about Daniel's God. And yet the fact that the king turned to Daniel last, shows he hadn't yet become a follower of the LORD.

Application – Sometimes, it takes many encounters with the Lord before a person is saved. Do not be discouraged if your initial efforts to share the good news with others aren't met with immediate results. Some seeds grow quickly. And some seeds grow more slowly. The seeds planted in Nebuchadnezzar's heart were the slow-growing kind. Yet they were growing, little by little.

Galatians 6:9 - *And let us not grow weary of doing good, for in due season we will reap, if we do not give up.*

2. The visions of my head – Nebuchadnezzar related the dream along with every detail he could remember. He had clearly seen these visions in his head as he lay in his bed.

Many times when we have a dream at night we can barely remember it in the morning. Or, if we do remember it, the details have fled, and only a fuzzy, vague impression remains.

Not so with this dream. The astonishing level of detail is one indicator that this was no normal dream. It was sent by God with a clear message for Nebuchadnezzar.

He seemed to sense that it was loaded with personal meaning. And that knowledge drove him to find out the answers to the riddle.

3. Nebuchadnezzar had confidence that Daniel could tell him the interpretation –

Proverbs 22:29 - *Do you see a man skillful in his work? He will stand before kings; he will not stand before obscure men.*

God had greatly blessed Daniel. One of the ways He blessed Daniel was by giving him the gift of interpretation. As Daniel continued to faithfully use his talents and gifts (given by God), he was given more opportunities and a bigger stage. With each new opportunity, Daniel once again proved faithful.

We are reminded that he who is faithful in a little thing (Daniel 1) is faithful also in much (Daniel 2,4,5,6).

Application – God has given you talents and gifts as well and He expects you to use these for building His kingdom. As you prove to be faithful in the small things, He will give you more opportunities.

- What is your gifting?
- If you don't know, how can you find out?
- How can you use your gifting to build God's kingdom this week?

IV. Daniel interprets the dream (19-27)

Discussion Questions

- Why do you think Daniel was appalled?

- What does this show about his relationship with Nebuchadnezzar?
- Do you think the latter part of verse 19 is genuine or just flattery?
- Does verse 22 remind you of any other prophetic condemnations (Nathan against David)?
- Why was Nebuchadnezzar going to face this punishment?
- What principle does this teach (pride goes before the fall and God's sovereignty)?
- Did you ever experience God humbling you when you were prideful?
- What advice did Daniel have for Nebuchadnezzar?
- Did he listen?

Cross-References

Psalms 119:46 – I will speak of your statutes before kings and not be put to shame.

Proverbs 28:13 - Whoever conceals his transgressions will not prosper, but he who confesses and forsakes them will obtain mercy.

Isaiah 55:6-7 - "Seek the Lord while he may be found; call upon him while he is near; let the wicked forsake his way, and the unrighteous man his thoughts; let him return to the Lord, that he may have compassion on him, and to our God, for he will abundantly pardon.

Ezekiel 18:21 - But if a wicked person turns away from all his sins that he has committed and keeps all my statutes and does what is just and right, he shall surely live; he shall not die.

Matthew 3:8 - Bear fruit in keeping with repentance.

Teaching Points

1. Daniel was dismayed – When Daniel heard the dream, he was very troubled. His emotion wasn't faked. He was clearly disturbed when he realized what was going to happen to the king, saying, "*My lord, may the dream be for those who hate you and its interpretation for your enemies!*"

This response gives us some insight into Daniel's character. Notably, he was loyal and cared for others. Most of the professional wise men class in Babylon cared only for themselves. What set Daniel apart was his care for the king. That was also a big reason his service was such an asset to the king. Daniel genuinely sought Nebuchadnezzar's well-being.

Application – Do you have this same loyalty to the people around you? If your boss was hit with bad news like this, how would you feel?

2. The dream and its interpretation – Daniel broke down the dream and its meaning for Nebuchadnezzar. The main idea was simple. Nebuchadnezzar and his kingdom had grown very powerful, its reach and influence extending across the earth. However, the king did not give credit to God. Therefore, he himself would be disciplined by God. He would be driven out from among men and become like a beast of the field for seven periods of time (perhaps years). But the discipline would be temporary. His kingdom would be held for him until he humbled himself. After that point in time, he could be restored.

One of the key themes in the book of Daniel is that God's kingdom is the only one that endures forever. Everything else, from the lowest person to the most powerful kingdom on earth, is temporary and will fade away.

Throughout this book, we have seen God teaching Nebuchadnezzar this lesson. But despite all of the miracles to this point, the king had not yet gotten the point. He was still prideful and credited himself for his great empire. In the end, God wins. Truth wins. Sooner or later, every person will learn the same lesson that the Lord sought to teach Nebuchadnezzar.

Application – Understand that this world and everything in it is temporary. Riches will not last. Do not set your hope on them. At the same time, what you do have is given to you by the Lord. Give Him full credit for everything good in your life. If you don't give glory to God and declare that your achievements are solely the result of your ingenuity and hard work, you are the same as Nebuchadnezzar. God gives grace to the humble but is opposed to the proud (1 Peter 5:5-6). If you have a good job, give glory to God. If you have a happy family, thank God for His blessings. If you have achieved something significant, acknowledge it was due to the abilities, gifts, and talents God gave to you first.

3. Daniel's counsel –

Daniel 4:27 - *Therefore, O king, let my counsel be acceptable to you: break off your sins by practicing righteousness, and your iniquities by showing mercy to the oppressed, that there may perhaps be a lengthening of your prosperity.*

I love this. Daniel is so bold and forthright. The king had asked for the interpretation, not for counsel. But Daniel gave both. His loyalty to the king and his role as God's messenger both compelled him to use this opportunity to speak the truth. The stage was not too big. Though Nebuchadnezzar was the most powerful man in the world (and had a notorious temper), it did not faze Daniel.

Reflect – What gave Daniel the confidence to boldly confront the king in this manner?

His trust was in the Lord. Daniel lived out the verse, "*If God is for me, who can be against me?*" (Romans 8:31)

Application – Do not let fear of man silence you when you should speak. Standing on the truth of God's word can strengthen you to courageously be the voice of wisdom. Is there a situation in your life you have been afraid to speak into? Is God calling you to speak up and say what needs to be said? Will you do it?

V. The dream is fulfilled (28-33)

Discussion Questions

- What event immediately brought God's punishment down?
- Is this a common problem for rich/powerful people?
- Is it a common problem for poor/not powerful people?
- How can we apply the lessons Nebuchadnezzar learned to our lives?
- What kind of condition did Nebuchadnezzar have? Is this a parable or an actual event? Why?

Cross-References

Numbers 23:19 - God is not man, that he should lie, or a son of man, that he should change his mind. Has he said, and will he not do it? Or has he spoken, and will he not fulfill it?

Teaching Points

1. All this came upon Nebuchadnezzar – God did just what He said He would do. The most powerful king the world had ever seen could not thwart God's sovereign will.

Application – Let know one think that he will be the one to escape God's justice.

2. Nebuchadnezzar pridefully gives himself the glory for his kingdom –

Daniel 4:30 - *Is not this great Babylon, which I have built by my mighty power as a royal residence and for the glory of my majesty?*

This happened twelve months after the initial dream. Most likely, the dream shocked Nebuchadnezzar. He had seen the divine hand of God many times, so he knew what God's power could accomplish. This knowledge and Daniel's counsel probably sparked something like a revival for Nebuchadnezzar. He would have been very pious and careful to demonstrate the appropriate attitude of humility.

However, traumatic events don't really change one's underlying character. Emotional-based responses are short-lived. And once the immediate danger seems past, people let their guard down again, and their fundamental nature takes over.

In the face of death, many people have promised to give their life to God if He will only save them. When the moment of danger is gone, most forget their promises and return to their previous ways. The same is true for many who face a health crisis. Some pray, "if only you will heal me, I will follow you." But after being healed, they forget God again.

Thus, twelve months later, after the initial adrenaline rush of piety, memories of the dream faded, and Nebuchadnezzar began boasting again. The gardens of Babylon are known as one of the seven wonders of the ancient world. And as he viewed those gardens, visions of his own splendor overcame him.

All credit for the beauty of his kingdom was assigned to himself. After all, God Himself had said that Nebuchadnezzar was the golden head!

Application – Develop a deep-rooted relationship with the Lord, one that will remain firm in the face of the emotional ups and downs of life. It is easy to reach a spiritual high after some amazing moment in your life. It is harder to maintain humility and an awareness of God's hand in your life in the day-to-day grind.

3. While the words were still in the king's mouth – God's justice was swift. There were no more warnings. The King of Kings had already issued His decree one year before. When Nebuchadnezzar refused to change his ways, God decided to humble him and teach him a lesson he would never forget.

4. God hates pride – One of the key lessons of this chapter is that the Lord hates pride. Rather than thankfully acknowledging God as the source of his success, Nebuchadnezzar exalted himself.

Whenever a person glorifies himself, he is stealing from God. Only God is worthy of our praise. Replacing him with anything else is blasphemy.

Many Scriptures attest to God's opposition toward the proud. One day every knee will bow, and every tongue will confess that Jesus is Lord.

Application – You can choose to bow, or you will be forced to. It's much more comfortable to choose to submit to God yourself.

5. Nebuchadnezzar became like an animal – Some scholars speculate that he was kept in the royal gardens during this period. Some doctors speculate that Nebuchadnezzar was afflicted with boanthropy, a disease in which the sufferer believes he is a cow or ox.

Whatever the scientific explanations are, God's hand was clearly behind it. God can use natural or supernatural means to accomplish His purposes. Both demonstrate His sovereign power.

VI. Nebuchadnezzar repents, is restored, and praises God (34-37)

Discussion Questions

- What was Nebuchadnezzar's response to the punishment?
- Do you think after this he finally learned his lesson?
- Do you think he was genuinely saved?

Cross-References

James 4:6-7 - But he gives more grace. Therefore it says, "God opposes the proud but gives grace to the humble." Submit yourselves therefore to God. Resist the devil, and he will flee from you.

1 Peter 5:5-6 - Likewise, you who are younger, be subject to the elders. Clothe yourselves, all of you, with humility toward one another, for "God opposes the proud but gives grace to the humble." Humble yourselves, therefore, under the mighty hand of God so that at the proper time he may exalt you,

Proverbs 3:34 - Toward the scorners he is scornful, but to the humble he gives favor.

Proverbs 29:23 - One's pride will bring him low, but he who is lowly in spirit will obtain honor.

Proverbs 16:18 - Pride goes before destruction, and a haughty spirit before a fall.

Teaching Points

1. Nebuchadnezzar was restored – Note when the king was restored. It was as soon as he "*lifted up [his] eyes to heaven.*" This was a tacit acknowledgment that God was sovereign. In his animal-like form, words were not possible. The only gesture Nebuchadnezzar could make to show his remorse was looking up at heaven. And his change of attitude is clearly seen in the following verses.

From this, we can see the mercy of God. His discipline was not one second longer than it needed to be. Nebuchadnezzar was disciplined for his own good. It was not punitive but loving and corrective.

Hebrews 12:6 - *For the Lord disciplines the one he loves, and chastises every son whom he receives.*

This discipline was evidence that God loved Nebuchadnezzar. God could have left him in his sin, but He didn't. Instead, He mercifully taught him the error of his ways and led him to confess.

Nebuchadnezzar was fully restored in mental faculty and power as his throne was returned to him.

2. Nebuchadnezzar finally glorifies God – This is the last we see of Nebuchadnezzar in the book of Daniel. And his story ends here on a very positive note. After multiple encounters with the Most High God, Nebuchadnezzar gives Him full glory. It is a beautiful testimony and a powerful proclamation.

This proclamation was sent to the entire kingdom. The brutal truth of what had happened painted King Nebuchadnezzar in a terrible light. He was exposed as arrogant. More than that, his weakness was exposed to his subjects. All could see that the king was not really in charge. There was a higher authority. Most leaders desperately try to cover this truth as they demand total allegiance. That is the same thing Nebuchadnezzar had done before, but no more!

Now the king publicly acknowledged God's authority, superiority, power, and sovereignty. He also finally learned the lesson of the book, which is that God's kingdom is the only one that endures forever.

Reflect – Was Nebuchadnezzar a real believer?

Application - Nebuchadnezzar learned the lesson. Have you? Do not love the world or the things in the world. All of it is fading. Humbly submit to the King of Kings. Wisely invest in His eternal kingdom. What is one way you can invest in His kingdom this week?

Daniel 5

Outline

I. The wild feast (1-4)
II. The handwriting on the wall (5-9)
III. The queen recommends Daniel (10-12)
IV. The king asks Daniel to interpret the writing (13-16)
V. Daniel preaches to the king (17-24)
VI. Daniel interprets the writing and is rewarded (25-29)
VII. The Babylonian kingdom falls (30-31)

I. The wild feast (1-4)

Discussion Questions

- What kind of feast do you think this was? What would have likely been going on there?
- What was going on outside the Babylonian walls at the time of this feast? (The Persians were sieging the city.)
- Why was Belshazzar feasting while the city was under attack?
- What is Belshazzar doing in verses 2-3?
- What attitude can you see from Belshazzar in these verses?
- Why do you think he specifically brought out the vessels from the Jewish temple to desecrate?

Cross-References

2 Kings 24:13-14 – [Nebuchadnezzar] carried off all the treasures of the house of the Lord and the treasures of the king's house, and cut in pieces all the vessels of gold in the temple of the Lord, which Solomon king of Israel had made, as the Lord had foretold. He carried away all Jerusalem and all the officials and all the mighty men of valor, 10,000 captives, and all the

craftsmen and the smiths.

Isaiah 42:8 - I am the Lord; that is my name; my glory I give to no other, nor my praise to carved idols.

Teaching Points

1. There were armies outside the city – The Medio-Persian army encircled the city, laying siege to it. While their enemies were invading, Belshazzar seemed oblivious, with little care for the goings on outside the city walls. Babylon was famous for its massive and seemingly impregnable walls. It was said to have twenty years of food and a water supply.

Thus the feast was likely partly due to Belshazzar's arrogance in thinking that they were invincible. At the same time, it may have been used to boost morale and defy the Persians.

Belshazzar would have better served his people by supervising the city defenses. But we see in him much of the same pride of Nebuchadnezzar.

2. Who is Belshazzar? – For a long time, skeptics dismissed the Biblical account listing Belshazzar as king in Babylon as unreliable since all other historical records stated Nabonidus was king. Not one single other record mentioned Belshazzar. Critics had found their ammunition to attack the Bible.

And the book of Daniel had a target on its back even more than other books in the Bible. In this book, Daniel made several prophecies about world events in astonishing detail. And they came true. Critics, therefore, had good reason to try to undermine the Biblical date of the authorship of Daniel and make it much later. If they could cast doubt on Daniel's credibility, they could explain away these prophecies as coming after the fact.

Their line of attack was simple. Daniel wrote his book much later and was unfamiliar with the actual history of the time. When Daniel wrote that Belshazzar was king, he made a critical mistake and exposed his prophecies as a fraud.

But Daniel's account (the only one with Belshazzar) was verified through archaeology, and their attacks against the Bible were thwarted. The Bible was once again shown to be reliable history.

Two important artifacts were discovered in 1854, the Nabonidus cylinder and tablet. These verified the Biblical account. One of these artifacts records Nabonidus' prayer to a moon good. In this record, he prays for "Belshazzar, the eldest son, my offspring."

On the other, it is recorded that Nabonidus left Babylon for a decade and left his son as "the crown prince" and "entrusted the kingship" to "his oldest (son) the firstborn." Thus he would not have been in Babylon at the time of the Persian invasion.

It is no wonder that Belshazzar could only make Daniel "third highest" (Daniel 5:16) in the kingdom after Nabonidus and himself! If Daniel had been written hundreds of years later (as critics claim), it is doubtful he would have known about this mysterious historical figure. Daniel was historically accurate because he was there. His prophecies were predictions of the future inspired by God.

Application – Skeptics will always seek to attack the veracity of God's word. When one attack fails, they will go on to the next. It is a never-ending cycle. The Bible outlasts every one of these attacks. Time and time again, archaeology has confirmed various Biblical accounts.

There will always be things in the Bible that cannot be proven through other historical records or archaeology since these events occurred thousands of years ago. However, our faith need not be shaken when doubts are raised about Scripture. It has proven itself to be reliable.

It may be that in our lifetimes more evidence will be uncovered that repels these attacks. Or it may be that certain things remain unknown. Since the Bible has proven reliable, we can have faith in it even in areas where there is no immediate answer.

To put it another way, you do not need to verify every word of your friend from another source in order to trust your friend. If your friend has shown himself to be truthful over time, that is enough to take "his word for it" rather than demanding video evidence that he actually went to MacDonalds for lunch yesterday.

2. Belshazzar defied the true God - Although Daniel and Nebuchadnezzar had been an influence, he showed that he wanted no part of this "Hebrew"

God. It wasn't enough for him to ignore God through his lifestyle and actions. He specifically called for the vessels from Solomon's temple so he could desecrate them publicly to show his contempt for the Lord. This was a calculated and planned ritual symbolic of his defiance of God. It was a foolish thing.

It's like a kid who is dared to light firecrackers on somebody's porch. All the kids nervously watch, wondering if he can do it. Finally, he does it and runs away, and all of them laugh at the joke together until the house owner comes and catches them.

Belshazzar was arrogant. While he should have been concerned with his city's defenses (and prayed to God for help!), he instead threw a party with the express purpose of taunting God!

3. These vessels were eventually returned to Jerusalem (Ezra 1:7-11).

4. Instead of praising the true God, they substituted idols –

People are spiritual and religious by nature. No one worships nothing. If someone doesn't worship the true God, they will worship something else, maybe money, maybe self, maybe a pagan religion, maybe strength or power, but they will most definitely worship something.

Romans 1:21-23 - *Although they knew God, they did not honor him as God or give thanks to him, but they became futile in their thinking, and their foolish hearts were darkened. Claiming to be wise, they became fools, and exchanged the glory of the immortal God for images resembling mortal man and birds and animals and creeping things.*

People substitute idols in place of God because they don't want God's authority. They want to be free and independent to do whatever they like without anyone telling them what to do. They want to have their cake and eat it too. They want a god to comfort, protect, and bless them, but they don't want a god they have to obey.

II. The handwriting on the wall (5-9)

Discussion Questions

- Whose fingers do you think this was?
- Why was the king so scared?
- What similarities can you see in his response and
- Nebuchadnezzar's response earlier to similar situations?
- Who did he turn to for help?

Cross-References

Job 20:5 - That the exulting of the wicked is short, and the joy of the godless but for a moment?

Proverbs 29:1 - He who is often reproved, yet stiffens his neck, will suddenly be broken beyond healing.

Luke 12:19-20 - And I will say to my soul, "Soul, you have ample goods laid up for many years; relax, eat, drink, be merry.'" But God said to him, Fool! This night your soul is required of you, and the things you have prepared, whose will they be?'

Teaching Points

1. Suddenly (Daniel 5:5 NASB)- Suddenly, at the height of Belshazzar's pride and defiance, God sent His judgment. Defiance of God never ends well. Just when the king thought everything was going great, he was surprised. God intervened. It often appears that the wicked will go unpunished and get away with their evil, and they sometimes do for a while. But eventually, often suddenly, God's judgment will fall and it will be too late to avoid it.

Psalms 73:17 - *Until I went into the sanctuary of God; then I discerned their (the wicked) end.*

In the book of Psalms, Asaph questions why the wicked seem to prosper. It confused him why they could defy God and get richer and more prosperous. The answer Asaph received was simple. In verse 17, he says, "then I perceived their end." He goes on to say, "you set them in slippery places. You cast them down to destruction. They are destroyed in a moment… utterly swept away by sudden terrors! Like a dream when one awakens."

Eventually, sooner or later, the wicked will receive justice for the wrongs they have done. They will not take their riches with them after death. One day each person will face God as the judge and have to give an account for everything he has done. The security that their riches seem to provide is short-lived. It is not real security at all.

While their lives seem smooth and easy, destruction comes upon them in a moment. Asaph's description reminds us of Jesus' parable about the rich fool, who did not know that he was about to die and that everything so carefully stored up would avail him nothing. Money is but for a moment. A life built on things of this world is on a slippery slope. Only a life built on the rock of Christ is safe and sound.

Belshazzar's life and his reign would suddenly end because of his pride.

Application - Do not be jealous of the wicked, their lives, or what they own! They and all they own will perish in the end!

2. The handwriting on the wall – The fingers of a human hand appeared and started writing on the wall. Belshazzar's bluster was gone. The miracle absolutely terrified him, draining the blood from his face and inducing his limbs to shake.

From his reaction, we can see that the bravado shown earlier was just a front to hide his insecurities and fear. Deep inside, I believe he knew God was real.

In like manner, the bluster of the loudest atheists is an attempt to bury the truth they know to be true; they are created by God.

3. The king turned to the ineffective diviners and wise men – Prince Belshazzar had likely heard the stories of God's miracles in the life of Nebuchadnezzar. But he didn't humble himself or seek after God. Neither did he search for Daniel, who had helped his grandfather so many times.

Instead, he went to the Babylonian wise men, who once again were unable to help.

Application – Make sure to turn to the right source for wisdom. If you go to this world, you will get worldly wisdom. If you go to the Lord, you will get heavenly wisdom.

3. He offered great promises of reward (5:7) - This was the system they dealt with. People did favors for the king because they wanted rewards or were afraid of punishment. Threats of punishment or promises of compensation are the tools used by the world. Even this didn't help as the wise men were puzzled.

They *"could not read the writing or make known to the king the interpretation."*

The world's wisdom is blind when it comes to the things of God.

1 Corinthians 2:14 - *The natural person does not accept the things of the Spirit of God, for they are folly to him, and he is not able to understand them because they are spiritually discerned.*

III. The queen suggests Daniel (10-12)

Discussion Questions

- Who might this queen have been?
- Why do you think Belshazzar did not know about Daniel?
- How old was Daniel when all of this happened?
- Why do you think Daniel was no longer around the palace scene?

Teaching Points

1. The queen recommends Daniel –

Many years have passed since the events of Daniel 1-4. It appears that his position is much less prominent than in the past. However, a queen knows about Daniel and recommends him to the king.

The queen may have been a young wife of Nebuchadnezzar or his daughter.

Daniel 5:11-12 - *There is a man in your kingdom in whom is the spirit of the holy gods. In the days of your father, light and understanding and wisdom like the wisdom of the gods were found in him, and King Nebuchadnezzar, your father—your father the king—made him chief of the magicians, enchanters, Chaldeans, and astrologers, because an excellent spirit, knowledge, and understanding to interpret dreams, explain riddles, and solve problems were found in this Daniel, whom the king named Belteshazzar. Now let Daniel be called, and he will show the interpretation."*

2. Nebuchadnezzar wasn't Belshazzar's direct father – Here, "father" is a term for ancestor and is often used that way in Scripture. Nebuchadnezzar would have been Belshazzar's grandfather.

3. It seems that when Belshazzar's administration took over, Daniel wasn't a significant part of it. Belshazzar probably purged Nebuchadnezzar's kingdom of the positive influences of the Most High, such as Daniel. Considering his public antagonism for the LORD, he probably reversed the decrees Nebuchadnezzar had made promoting the worship of God. His attitude shows defiance of the Lord. And in this atmosphere, Daniel would not have been welcome. Another possibility is that Daniel himself largely withdrew from the active affairs of government because of his age or the evil policies of Belshazzar.

5. Daniel's influence profoundly impacted many people, including the queen. He had been very visible and influential as a witness of God for a long time. We see that here there is some fruit of that.

IV. The king asks Daniel to interpret the writing (13-16)

Discussion Question

- Why would Daniel be made the "third ruler"?

1. Belshazzar uses rewards to try to motivate Daniel – This is a window into his heart. To him, wealth and luxury were all-important. So it is natural to him that others would be motivated by the same things.

2. The king offers Daniel the third-highest ranking in the kingdom. That was the highest possible position available behind Nabonidus and Belshazzar.

3. Daniel was the last choice, not the first choice.

V. Daniel preaches to the king (17-24)

Discussion Questions

- Why would Daniel not take the gifts?
- Can you think of anyone else in the Bible that would not take gifts?
- Should we take gifts from evil people?
- What did Daniel do before interpreting the writing?
- What story did he tell Belshazzar and what was his main point?
- What can we see about Daniel's attitude in front of Belshazzar?
- What can we learn from this?
- Do you think it is a coincidence the hand appeared right at the climax of the king's pride and defiance of the Lord? Why do you think it happened then?

Cross-References

Proverbs 17:27 - Whoever restrains his words has knowledge, and he who has a cool spirit is a man of understanding.

Luke 18:14 - I tell you, this man went down to his house justified, rather than the other. For everyone who exalts himself will be humbled, but the one who humbles himself will be exalted."

Proverbs 16:5 - Everyone who is arrogant in heart is an abomination to the Lord; be assured, he will not go unpunished.

Isaiah 26:10 - If favor is shown to the wicked, he does not learn righteousness; in the land of uprightness he deals corruptly and does not see the majesty of the Lord.

Teaching Points

1. Let your gifts be for yourself - Daniel, like Abraham before, refused to take the gifts. His refusal demonstrated that materials and rewards were not important to him. He wasn't like the others. Daniel wasn't motivated by the things that motivated others. His concern was truth, righteousness, and accurately conveying God's messages.

2. Daniel took the opportunity to preach – At this point, Daniel was likely around eighty-five years old. He was an old man and had been away from the king's court for a long time. The scene around him was wild revelry. The ruler before him was unstable and unhinged. Belshazzar held the Lord in outright contempt. It was a dangerous situation and one wrong word could condemn Daniel to the king's fury.

But Daniel wasn't fazed. Instead of cowering, he took advantage of this grand opportunity to preach to the king and, by extension, the entire court.

Imagine that you get called into a chaotic bar scene where the leader of your country awaits a word with you. Would you start sharing the gospel then and there?

That is what Daniel did.

2 Timothy 4:2 - *Preach the word; be ready in season and out of season; reprove, rebuke, and exhort, with complete patience and teaching.*

Reflect – Was this in season or out of season to preach the word?

Application – Be bold. Like Daniel, we should always look for opportunities to speak the truth from God into others' lives. No stage is too big (or too small). Preach the word in season and out of season.

3. Daniel reviewed the history of God's work in Nebuchadnezzar's life-

After an oral review of the lessons God taught to the Babylonians through the life of Nebuchadnezzar, Daniel's preaching centers directly on Belshazzar before him. The highlight is found in verses 22-23.

Daniel 5:22-23 - *And you his son, Belshazzar, have not humbled your heart, though you knew all this, but you have lifted up yourself against the Lord of heaven. And the vessels of his house have been brought in before you, and you and your lords, your wives, and your concubines have drunk wine from them. And you have praised the gods of silver and gold, of bronze, iron, wood, and stone, which do not see or hear or know, but the God in whose hand is your breath, and whose are all your ways, you have not honored.*

Wow. Talk about boldness! Daniel holds no punches. To paraphrase this message, Daniel tells the ruler, "You are prideful and rebellious!"

For over seventy years, Daniel was faithful in serving as God's messenger. He did so in a dark and dangerous place with little care for his own life. And through it all, God protected him.

Reflect – Have you ever been in a high-pressure situation like Daniel's with an opportunity to witness? How did you react?

VI. Daniel interprets the writing and is rewarded (25-29)

Discussion Questions

- How is this similar to the judgment every person will go through?
- What prophesy/prophecies did this fulfill?

Cross-References

Job 31:6 - Let me be weighed in a just balance, and let God know my integrity!

Jeremiah 25:13, 44, 50, 51, 52,57, Isaiah 13, 47, Habakkuk 2:5-19 – A list of prophecies against Babylon.

Teaching Points

1. The writing on the wall said, "Mene, Mene, Tekel, and Parsin." –

This is how Daniel interpreted the meaning:

A. God has numbered the days of your kingdom.

B. You have been weighed in the balances and found wanting.

C. Your kingdom is divided and given to the Medes and Persians.

Simply put, Belshazzar and his kingdom would be punished because they were prideful and didn't trust the Lord.

Reflect – How would your life hold up if it was weighed by the Lord's divine scales?

Application – We also would be found wanting. No one can live up to God's standards. No one can pass the test. Our only hope is to humble ourselves and come to Christ at the cross. His righteousness imputed to us can fill up what we are lacking. Then when God weighs us, Jesus' righteousness will be weighed on our behalf. Instead of thinking you are good enough, be humble and admit you are not.

2. This time, Daniel doesn't seem sorry or upset as he was when he found out Nebuchadnezzar would be punished (Daniel 4:19). He doesn't have the same close relationship with Belshazzar that he had with his grandfather.

3. The punishment was sent when Belshazzar's pride reached a climax.

Proverbs 16:18 - *Pride goes before destruction, and a haughty spirit before a fall.*

4. Every kingdom in the history of the world has been found wanting - None of them have been perfect, and most have degenerated into being very evil and corrupt.

The only kingdom that will never be found wanting is Christ's kingdom, which will be a permanent one.

Application - Don't place your faith in your country or political leaders. These are all lacking in God's sight.

5. Sometimes if you don't want gifts, God will see to it that you still get them – Daniel did not want the gifts. He did not serve for the rewards. They were frivolous and unnecessary for him. And yet he still received the gifts as well as a promotion.

Application – Material reward should never be our primary motivation. Trust in God's provision. If you seek His kingdom and righteousness first, He will provide all the things you need.

VII. The Babylonian kingdom falls (30-31)

Discussion Questions

- How did the city of Babylon finally fall?
- What does this teach us about God and man?

Teaching Points

1. History tells us the city fell through a brilliant military strategy of diverting the Euphrates so that they could go into the city under the walls. In most places, the walls were impregnable. But in one spot, the Euphrates flowed under the wall.

By lowering the water level, the Persian and Mede armies could go into the city under the fortifications instead of forcing their way through.

Persian accounts say that the city then surrendered without a fight. But ancient accounts are not in complete agreement on this detail.

2. The miraculous "one-day" defeat of the impregnable city was brought about by God.

3. Babylon fell as fast as it rose up –

God had used it to accomplish His purposes. Now its task of punishing Israel was done, and it would be punished in turn.

In the book of Habakkuk, the prophet is confused. He doesn't understand why God would use a wicked nation to judge Israel.

God's answer was that after He used Babylon to accomplish His purposes, they too would be judged for their sin. The rise and fall of Babylon (and all other kingdoms) reminds us of God's sovereignty. He is bringing His plan for the world to completion. And His kingdom is the only one that will endure forever.

4. The king died the same night.

Application – This chapter is a reminder that the things of the world are temporary. Those who put their trust in things, whether their power, money, or own intelligence, will be disappointed. All of the things we see around us will fade away.

Isaiah 40:8 - *The grass withers, the flower fades, but the word of our God will stand forever.*

Daniel 6

Outline

I. A righteous person is a good testimony (1-3)
II. A righteous person will face opposition (4-9)
III. A righteous person boldly stands on his convictions (10-16)
IV. A righteous person is never abandoned by God (17-24)
V. A righteous person makes a difference for the Lord (25-28)

I. A righteous person is a good testimony (1-3)

Discussion Questions

* Why do you think Daniel was appointed to such a high position in the new administration?
* What are the marks of a good employee?
* How is your reputation at your workplace?
* How can you become a better employee?

Cross-References

1 Peter 2:13-16 - Be subject for the Lord's sake to every human institution, whether it be to the emperor as supreme, or to governors as sent by him to punish those who do evil and to praise those who do good. For this is the will of God, that by doing good you should put to silence the ignorance of foolish people. Live as people who are free, not using your freedom as a cover-up for evil, but living as servants of God.

Teaching Points

1. Daniel's shining reputation –

Daniel is now probably a little over 80 years old. He served in a high position in Nebuchadnezzar's kingdom. Then he served in a high position in Belshazzar's kingdom. Both of these were Babylonian kings.

In Daniel 5, we learned about the overthrow of Babylon. Persia almost miraculously conquered this powerful capital in one night. It would be expected that the new foreign king would bring in his own officials and get rid of the previous administration. And yet Darius chose to have Daniel as one of three rulers he set over the entire kingdom.

Reflect - Why would the conquering king establish Daniel in such a prominent position?

Evidently, Daniel had a very good reputation. He was known as a person full of integrity. He was known as a wise, faithful, and loyal leader. The king wanted to find rulers who would protect his interests so that he *"might not suffer loss"* (verse 2.) Daniel fit the bill. And thus, he served as a top official in at least three administrations spanning six decades. Daniel was a good employee with a good testimony. Employing Daniel brought real value to his employers.

Application - Are you a good employee like Daniel? Do you have integrity as he did? Do you faithfully serve your boss' interests? As Daniel did, we work for bosses who are often not believers. We work for companies that do not honor God. How can we serve God while still being good employees?

From a worldly perspective (your bosses' perspective), a Christian employee has both some negative and positive sides. The negative is that the Christian employee will not blindly obey everything, even the sinful things he is asked to do.

The Christian accountant should not be willing to change the numbers. The Christian salesman should not be willing to exaggerate how good the product is. The employee who loves Jesus should not be a slave to his work, which would be a lower priority than his family.

If your boss only sees the negative side, you will not last long in your job. But there is a positive side too. An employee who follows Jesus should be trustworthy. That means he will be honest with his boss and company. Just as he will not cheat the customer, he will not cheat the company either. Good employees should arrive on time and work hard.

Once I noticed a program on CBS Sport's website for watching the NCAA Men's Basketball Tournament that takes place every March. One of the advertised features of this program was that it had a "Boss Button." The boss button allowed the watcher to close the video screen and open a fake spreadsheet at the click of a button. It was designed to encourage people to watch while at work. But to do this in secret without permission is stealing from the company.

A Christian employee should work hard even while the boss is out of the room.

Daniel kept being promoted because he was a faithful employee and served the interests of the king.

While other officials served their own interests and selfishly pursued personal gain, Daniel would not be corrupted. He was honest with his superiors and told them the cold, hard truth.

A follower of Jesus makes a good employee. It is not a guarantee that you will be promoted like Daniel was. And yet, if you are a good employee and work hard and behave with integrity, it is very likely that you will be successful.

Proverbs 22:29 - *The one skilled in his work will serve before kings.*

II. A righteous person will face opposition (4-9)

Discussion Questions

- Why did the other rulers seek to accuse him?
- What did their investigation uncover?
- What can we learn about Daniel's character from their failure? Do you think if people carefully examined you, they could find grounds for accusing you?
- Would they find that you are "too" devoted to the Lord from the world's perspective?
- Do unbelievers in the world today seek to accuse believers?
- Why or why not?
- How did they deceive the king?
- In what ways did they influence the king to pass this law?
- Is this an effective way to make a petition to an authority?

- Should we use this method?
- Why could the laws of the Medes and Persians not be changed? Is this a good idea to have a rule that a law cannot be changed? Why or why not?

Cross-References

Psalms 37:12-13 - The wicked plots against the righteous and gnashes his teeth at him, but the Lord laughs at the wicked, for he sees that his day is coming.

Psalms 37:32-33 - The wicked watches for the righteous and seeks to put him to death. The LORD will not abandon him to his power or let him be condemned when he is brought to trial.

Ecclesiastes 4:4 - Then I saw that all toil and all skill in work come from a man's envy of his neighbor. This also is vanity and a striving after wind.

Philippians 2:15 - Be blameless and innocent, children of God without blemish in the midst of a crooked and twisted generation, among whom you shine as lights in the world.

1 Peter 3:16-17 - Having a good conscience, so that, when you are slandered, those who revile your good behavior in Christ may be put to shame. For it is better to suffer for doing good, if that should be God's will, than for doing evil.

Teaching Points

1. Jealousy motivated these politicians to scheme against Daniel –

1 Peter 5:8 - *Be sober-minded; be watchful. Your adversary the devil prowls around like a roaring lion, seeking someone to devour.*

Do you know who Satan wants to devour the most? He wants to devour believers who have good testimonies. A good testimony for the Lord is a powerful tool to draw others to himself. A believer with a good testimony is like a lighthouse bringing ships in through a storm to a safe harbor. Satan wants to put out the light. His first method is often to tempt believers and get them to fall away. We saw this back in Daniel 1 when Daniel and his friends were tempted by unlawful food. When that doesn't work, his next method is often to get rid of the person to extinguish their light.

Notice in this passage that all of these other officials were united against Daniel. Together they went to the king and requested a new law, a law forbidding prayer to anyone except for him for 30 days. There were a total of 120 satraps and three administrators. One hundred twenty-two of them stood against Daniel. Not one spoke up in his defense. Not one disagreed with their plan. These were career politicians. Many of them surely hated each other's guts.

Reflect – What motivated them to plot against Daniel?

They are all jockeying for position. Each one wants to move higher up the chain. Make no mistake, they are not friends, not in normal circumstances. And yet here they are all united. This is the work of the enemy. A believer with a strong testimony will attract opposition from many sides.

2 Timothy 3:12 - *Indeed, all who desire to live a godly life in Christ Jesus will be persecuted.*

Did you know that persecution is promised? If you live for God, you will be opposed. A lot of believers like to claim God's promises. Did you ever claim the promise of persecution? It may not be our favorite one, but it is there to prepare us so that we will be ready when that moment comes.

If we are not prepared and are caught by surprise, we might not have the resolve or perseverance to face that persecution and endure. Much of the battle takes place before the actual moment of persecution.

Opposition may come from different sources. It could be a parent who is opposed to the gospel. It could be co-workers who are out to get you. It could be a government that is hostile to believers. Or it could be persecution from the majority people group in your country. Know that if you live a godly life for the Lord, you will be opposed. If you never face this, it is possible you are too much like the world.

Reflect - How can you prepare ahead to face persecution?

Application – Do not be surprised when you are persecuted for the gospel. Dig your root deep into Christ and His Word so that when persecutions come, you will have a solid foundation. Practicing standing up for right in everyday choices will help strengthen you so that you will not compromise when bigger tests come your way.

2. Daniel was blameless. -

We know that Daniel publicly was a good and faithful employee with a good testimony. What about his private life? We see a powerful statement about Daniel's character in verse 4.

Daniel 6:4 - *Then the high officials and the satraps sought to find a ground for complaint against Daniel with regard to the kingdom, but they could find no ground for complaint or any fault, because he was faithful, and no error or fault was found in him.*

These people tried every method of spying on Daniel's secrets. Their investigations would have included checking his projects and paperwork, asking questions of his co-workers, and examining his house and possessions.

Throughout history, political adversaries have been very good at bringing out the secret sins of their opponents. Most investigations can turn up plenty of dirt because, as the saying goes, "everyone has a skeleton in their closet." Well, Daniel didn't.

Although they tried as hard as they could, they could find nothing even remotely shady in Daniel's personal or professional life. In fact, the only thing they could find to accuse him of was that he was too zealous in his service to God (5)! He was too faithful to God! Wow! Isn't that amazing?

Daniel had a shining testimony. It wasn't an act. It wasn't faked. He wasn't one person at the office and another person at home. He wasn't one person at church and another person in front of his friends. He wasn't one person on Sunday and another person on the rest of the week. Daniel was the real deal. This is who he was. He was a righteous person who lived like it no matter where he was or who was watching.

Application - Put yourself in Daniel's place for a moment. Imagine that a team of detectives investigates your life. Their goal is to dig out your secret sins. They want to expose you. They want to prove that you are a different person during the week than on Sundays. So they dig into every aspect of your life. What will they find?

If they were to check your credit card bills and banking account history, what would they find you spend money on? What will they find out about your truthfulness in paying taxes? If they were to look at your internet browsing history, what would they see there? If they were to check out the movies you watch, the music you listen to, or the books you read when no one else is around, what would they discover? If they were to observe how you treated your family members and recorded a video of it, would you want to play it in church on Sunday?

If they had the ability to go even deeper and record the thoughts you think when you are all alone, what would they find? What would the final report be?

Think for a moment about what you would be most afraid of them finding. Brothers and sisters, if you could think of anything, then today, take it to the Lord. Repent. God can help you be righteous. God can help you have a testimony as pure and blameless as Daniel's. A person of integrity and righteousness can live with no fear of being caught.

Titus 2:7-8 - *Show yourself in all respects to be a model of good works, and in your teaching show integrity, dignity, and sound speech that cannot be condemned, so that an opponent may be put to shame, having nothing evil to say about us.*

3. Lessons from the officials' interaction with King Darius –

From these verses, we are reminded of two things that we should not do.

A. We should not use flattery and manipulation to achieve what we want as these officials did. Also, we should not let ourselves be manipulated by flattery. You can see a clear difference in this book between Daniel, who talks straight with the kings, and these wise men who slant everything to suit their own purposes.

B. We should not make promises without thinking them through very carefully. The king made a grave mistake in accepting their deal without taking proper care to consider its ramifications.

4. They lied to the king, saying that they had all agreed – This was not true as Daniel had not agreed to the plan.

5. They proposed to make a man a god for thirty days - Their idea was to make Darius a god for 30 days simply by royal decree. Such an idea would have been sure to appeal to Darius' ego. After all, his loyal subjects clearly adored him so much that it was only right that he blessed them with the opportunity to show their sincere affection!

These officials knew how to manipulate the king by stroking his vanity and ego. Today such a law seems insane and likely to invite immediate revolt. However, in the ancient world, it was common for emperors to be worshiped as deities.

Application – As Jesus told Satan, worship the Lord your God and serve Him only (Luke 4:8). Some governments demand a near worship level of devotion. And in Revelation, we learn that is the way the world will be going in the end times. Indeed, there is nothing new under the sun. Throughout history, one of Satan's most tried methods of attack is to get people to replace God with another object of worship: idol, self, money, hobby, evolution, or a person. Is there someone or something in your life vying for your highest allegiance?

III. A righteous person boldly stands on his convictions (10-16)

Discussion Questions

- Did Daniel change any of his habits after he heard the law was passed?
- Why not?
- What does this reveal about his character?
  What would you do if this law was passed today?
- When did the king realize his mistake?
- What could he do about it?
- What can we learn from this about how laws should or shouldn't be passed and the structure of government?
- What can we learn about how decisions should or shouldn't be made?

Cross-References

Luke 14:26 - If anyone comes to me and does not hate his own father and mother and wife and children and brothers and sisters, yes, and even his own life, he cannot be my disciple.

1 Kings 8:48 - If they repent with all their heart and with all their soul in the land of their enemies, who carried them captive, and pray to you toward their land, which you gave to their fathers, the city that you have chosen, and the house that I have built for your name.

Psalms 95:6 - Oh come, let us worship and bow down; let us kneel before the LORD, our Maker!

Acts 5:29 - But Peter and the apostles answered, "We must obey God rather than men.

Teaching Points

1. Daniel stands firm - What does Daniel do when he hears about the decree? The same thing he always does! Daniel does not change at all. He doesn't compromise his faith. He doesn't hide.

You always have a choice. No one can make you sin. The story of Daniel proves it is true. Once again, it looks like Daniel had no choice. Before, he was a young teenager standing up against the most powerful king in the world. Now he is a frail old man once again standing up against the most powerful king in the world. Most people his age would just want to live out the rest of their days in peace.

I don't believe Daniel did this with the goal of making a statement. It wasn't done in anger or pride. He did it simply because it was who he was. He wouldn't and couldn't change his very nature. He had been praying this way for decades. So for him to do it again was the most normal and natural thing in the world.

2. Daniel didn't change his behavior and then try to justify it - Daniel could have justified changing his routine just for these thirty days. After all, a person can pray anywhere, right? A person can pray with his eyes open. A person can pray with the door shut. Daniel could have simply gone to bed

and shut his eyes, and prayed silently before sleeping. No one could have possibly known. No one could have accused him. He could have avoided the wrath of the king. He could have avoided the accusations of the other officials. He could have kept his job and ability to influence people in the future. And it would have been so easy to do that. He certainly knew he could have done these things, but he still prayed in front of an open window facing Jerusalem.

Reflect – Why didn't Daniel choose a less confrontational way to worship God for these thirty days? Would it have been right for Daniel to change his routine and pray secretly for 30 days until the decree expired? Why or why not?

Daniel was a man of conviction. Changing his routine would have appeared to be a compromise because it was. He would have lost his testimony and moral authority. It is likely that Daniel's influence was instrumental in the decree soon after this allowing the Jews to return to Judah after the seventy-year captivity. While we know God is sovereign, we can also see that the decisions we make are important and have far-reaching consequences far beyond what we can even see.

James 4:17 - *So whoever knows the right thing to do and fails to do it, for him it is sin.*

We can learn three things about Daniel from his actions here:

A. He was bold. He did this in front of an open window without letting fear of the consequences stop him.

B. He had faith. Every time in the past that he took a leap of faith, God caught him. He had lived his entire life up to this point with faith in God, trusting that God would take care of him. And each time, God did. Thus his faith grew stronger and stronger. He knew that God was more powerful than any earthly king. And he knew that God would be with him again. For you too, when you take a leap of faith, God will show Himself faithful, and your faith will be increased for the next time.

C. He had conviction. Daniel had a clear sense of right and wrong. He didn't let the fads or opinions of the day sway him. But he stood straight and firm, unflinching because he knew he was standing on the truth.

Application - Are you a person of conviction? We need to carefully study the Scriptures and build up a foundation of principles on which we will stand no matter what. Many of these convictions will be very different from the world's opinions. They will be tested and opposed. But a conviction is a strong belief in your heart that you should not compromise no matter what others say.

I was blessed with parents who had strong convictions and taught me to have the same.

Once my father agreed to an odd job of building a fence for a customer at a certain price. When he started working on it, he realized the entire lot had bedrock just beneath the dirt's surface. Building the fence required digging numerous posts through solid rock. It took him far more time than he had calculated. In addition, he had to rent a jackhammer. It ended up costing him more than he made. But he had made a promise, so he kept it. That example has served to motivate me to this day.

I would encourage you to be a person of conviction. First, be clear in your mind about right and wrong. And then stand firm on the truth no matter what opposition you face. Your actions, right or wrong, will reflect back to God.

3. The king did not properly think through the ramifications before issuing this new law –

Proverbs 18:13 - *If one gives an answer before he hears, it is his folly and shame.*

Proverbs 20:25 - *It is a snare to say rashly, "It is holy," and to reflect only after making vows.*

Application – Do not make rash promises. Do not sign contracts without reading them. Do not make important decisions because of pressure put on you. Take the time to think, pray, and ask counsel first. Many disasters can be avoided by slowing down before making a promise.

4. The Persian law that laws couldn't be changed was ill-conceived – Likely, this law existed because of an incorrect belief that the king was infallible. If the king never made a mistake, then why allow a law to be changed?

The inherent pride and ego in this law are clearly evident. Everyone makes mistakes. It would be wise to allow for some method of repealing a law that is later shown to need changing.

Application – It is better not to make guarantees if you can avoid it. Instead, say that you "plan" to do something or will "probably" get it done. Or you can say, "if it is the Lord's will, I will do this or that." (James 4:15)

IV. A righteous person is never abandoned by God (17-24)

Discussion Questions

- Why was Daniel not eaten?
- How could this happen?
- Why do you think Daniel defended himself after the fact, not before?
- What happened to his accusers?
- What principle does this illustrate?
- What does this show about the miraculous nature of Daniel's deliverance?

Cross-References

Psalms 34:7 - The angel of the LORD encamps around those who fear him, and delivers them.

Hebrews 11:33 - Who through faith conquered kingdoms, enforced justice, obtained promises, stopped the mouths of lions.

Isaiah 3:10 - Tell the righteous that it shall be well with them, for they shall eat the fruit of their deeds.

Galatians 6:8 - For the one who sows to his own flesh will from the flesh reap corruption, but the one who sows to the Spirit will from the Spirit reap eternal life.

Proverbs 28:10 - Whoever misleads the upright into an evil way will fall into his own pit, but the blameless will have a goodly inheritance.

Teaching Points

1. God did not forsake Daniel - Daniel was forsaken by the king, who felt he had no choice but to follow the law and have Daniel thrown to the lions. However, he was never abandoned by God. These were lions that were purposefully starved in order to make them as ravenous as possible. Yet they didn't open their mouths to kill Daniel.

He says in verse 22 that God sent his angel to *"shut the mouth of the lions."*

Daniel does not sound the least surprised. And why should he be? God is in the business of doing miracles. He miraculously caused Daniel and his friends to look healthier after only ten days in chapter 1. He miraculously gave Daniel the interpretation of Nebuchadnezzar's two dreams in chapters 2 and 4. He miraculously delivered Daniel's friends from the fiery furnace in chapter 3. And he miraculously wrote on the wall and prophesied the downfall of the Babylonian kingdom in chapter 5. What are a few lions to God?

2. The lions' den was not a scene from a children's storybook –

Some pictures portray the lion's den as a pretty little place with light streaming in and Daniel pleasantly conversing with the lions or using them as a pillow. The lions' den was not that pleasant. It was meant to be a place of torture and death. It was likely dark, rank, and filled with human bones. It was designed to be frightening. The text describes a stone rolled over and placed on top. So likely, there were no windows either.

The scene makes us recall the words of David hundreds of years before in Psalm 23:4, *"Even though I walk through the darkest valley, I will fear no evil, for you are with me; your rod and your staff, they comfort me."*

Application - As God did not abandon Daniel to the lions, He will not abandon you either. God is still doing miracles. He still intervenes on behalf of His people. No matter what dark valley you need to go through, God is there with you. No matter how lonely and abandoned you feel, God will never leave you or forsake you. No matter who stops loving you, God will never stop loving you.

3. Daniel is vindicated –

Daniel 6:21-22 - *Then Daniel said to the king, "O king, live forever! My God sent his angel and shut the lions' mouths, and they have not harmed me, because I was found blameless before him; and also before you, O king, I have done no harm."*

Daniel knew that defense was useless beforehand. The law couldn't be changed. He was not going to apologize or make any excuses. Afterward, he was vindicated and took the opportunity to use his influence to reach out to the king, preach God's saving power, and remind the king of his loyalty to him and even more to God.

V. A righteous person makes a difference for the Lord (24-28)

Discussion Questions

- How did God use Daniel in the life of Darius?

Teaching Points

1. Daniel's enemies are punished – The ones who conspired against Daniel were punished in exactly the same way they had desired for Daniel. The outcome reinforces the Biblical principles that you reap what you sow (Galatians 6:8, Proverbs 28:10).

Certainly, it was good for the kingdom to get these officials out of leadership who so opposed God. He also had their families killed.

Take note of an important rule of biblical interpretation. Recording the historical narrative of what happened is not an endorsement. The Mosaic law specifically forbids children from being punished for their parent's sins and vice-versa.

Application – Sow the right types of seeds in your family, work, church, and neighborhood. When you do, you will reap a blessed and fruitful harvest.

2. Darius made a decree honoring God -

Only days before, this king had proudly declared himself to be a god. He demanded prayer from his subjects and forbade prayer to anyone or anything else. And yet now he does a complete 180-degree turn, commanding his subjects to fear and revere the "God of Daniel." He proclaims that Daniel's God is the "living God" and that His kingdom will last forever, unlike his own kingdom, which he knew was temporary. He ascribes miracles to God. Not only was the king himself convinced of this. But he issues a decree proclaiming this for circulation throughout the whole kingdom.

Because of one man's conviction and refusal to compromise, a beacon of light is shown for the entire kingdom to see. How many lives were touched and changed because of Daniels' firm faith? It's almost countless.

Not only were many lives changed then, but lives are also still being changed now, almost 2600 years later. Many scholars believe that the magi who went to visit Jesus after His birth were familiar with the Old Testament Scriptures and Yahweh largely because of Daniel's influence in the Persian kingdom.

Application –

When you make a stand for God, it will also make a difference. Firstly, it will help you to grow in your own spiritual journey. Beyond that, it will be a light to the people around you. Small actions of obedience to God can make a great difference in His kingdom. In what area do you need to make a stand for God?

Daniel 7

Outline

I. Daniel's vision of the four beasts (1-8)
II. The Ancient of Days reigns (9-12)
III. The Son of Man's kingdom (13-14)
IV. Interpretation of the vision (15-18)
V. The fourth beast and the antichrist (19-28)

I. Daniel's vision of the four beasts (1-8)

Discussion Questions

- Is this chapter in chronological order? When do these events occur?
- What key word or words are repeated in this chapter?
- In what way is writing down the dream helpful?
- What other Biblical passages describe a similar scene?
- What do you think of when you think of a beast? What qualities does a beast have?
- What type of animals did the four beasts appear as?
- What qualities can you see of these beasts from their descriptions?
- Would you want to make friends with these beasts? Why or why not?
- Why do you think that these kings are described in this way?

Cross-References

Revelation 13:1-2 - And I saw a beast rising out of the sea, with ten horns and seven heads, with ten diadems on its horns and blasphemous names on its heads. And the beast that I saw was like a leopard; its feet were like a bear's, and its mouth was like a lion's mouth. And to it the dragon gave his power and his throne and great authority.

Revelation 13:5-7 - And the beast was given a mouth uttering haughty and blasphemous words, and it was allowed to exercise authority for forty-two months. It opened its mouth to utter blasphemies against God, blaspheming his name and his dwelling, that is, those who dwell in heaven. Also it was allowed to make war on the saints and to conquer them. And authority was given it over every tribe and people and language and nation.

Teaching Points

1. In the first year of Belshazzar, king of Babylon – Daniel 5 records the last day and death of Belshazzar and chapter 6 records Daniel's ministry as official to the Persian king. Chapter 7 takes place at least ten years before these events.

At this time, it appears that Daniel had retired from active service at the court. But he didn't spend his days vacationing at the beach and collecting shells. Daniel was active as a prophet receiving and recording revelations from the Lord.

In the first six chapters of Daniel, he interprets the dreams of others. In the last six chapters, he himself is the recipient of special revelation from God. And while the first half of the book is a chronological history of Daniel's official service, the last half is more akin to a journal of his own interactions with the Lord.

Application – Believers should never retire from serving the Lord. As you grow older, the location and method of your ministry may change, but you should still minister. This truth is built on the principle that every aspect of our lives, from start to finish, belongs to the Lord.

2. Then he wrote down the dream and told the sum of the matter – Daniel faithfully recorded his dream and subsequent encounter with the heavenly being. His record was vital not only for his own memory and walk with the Lord but for us as well.

Application – We are to be diligent in our walk with the Lord. One way we can follow Daniel's example is to take good notes when we study the Word. Whether you are listening to a sermon, having a quiet time, or joining an inductive Bible study, you will get more out of it if you record what you are learning.

3. Four beasts came out of the sea – We see the same wording in Revelation regarding the rise of the beasts in the end times. The sea seems to be symbolic of the evil of mankind spread over the world. Sometimes it refers to Gentile nations (Psalm 74:13, Isiah 57:20). In Revelation 21:1, we learn that in the new earth there will be "no more sea." Man's evil system will be defeated. Evil plots will no longer be hatched against the Almighty.

When something is in the sea, it is hidden. Only when it comes out is it revealed. Therefore no one would be able to identify the identity of these beasts (kings) until after they were revealed by coming to power. Just as it would be folly to star at the surface of the water and guess at the location and identity of an unseen sea creature, so it would be to guess the names of these kings before they rose to power.

It could also relate to the Mediterranean Sea, as each of these four empires had a geographical connection to it.

4. The four beasts – Each of these beasts had a specific appearance. That is, each of these kingdoms which are described had unique features. They were four separate and distinct nations. And yet they also had similarities. The most obvious similarity is that each one was a beast.

The term beast generally has a negative connotation. Beasts generally are ugly (think Beauty and the Beast). Only the most powerful animals or mythical creatures are called beasts. But more than just their power, beasts are typified by a total lack of self-control. They lack any type of grace, morality, or culture. Instead, their actions are controlled by their basest instincts. Whereas a man has self-will and should restrain certain fleshly instincts, a beast never does. A beast is controlled by rage, passion, desire, and violence. To call a person a beast is a great insult. It means that he is behaving like a wild animal and not a man. Whereas a man is made in the image of God and is to live out the fruit of the Spirit, a beast has no soul and commits all the works of the flesh.

Therefore the term beast here shows us the depraved and lawless nature of these four kingdoms. They are like wild animals fulfilling their own passions. They have no desire to seek after God and live to satisfy the flesh.

In addition, these beasts were frightening to look at. They were destructive. A beast does not bring anything of value to the table. It only destroys. Like father like son. Satan also seeks only to kill and destroy.

97

John 10:10 - *The thief comes only to steal and kill and destroy. I came that they may have life and have it abundantly.*

The beasts act just like their father, the devil.

Jesus contrasted Himself with Satan. He brings abundant life. Jesus is a life-giving force. He offers the bread of life. He offers living water. Everything good and perfect is a gift from Him above.

The world, on the other hand, seeks to ensnare and ruin you. The nations and the systems of culture they espouse today are more akin to beasts than they are to God.

Would it be wise to go and cuddle with a bear? One man thought so. Timothy Treadwell and his girlfriend Amie Huguenard attempted to live with brown bears in Alaska. They made documentaries of their experiences, in which they claimed to build mutual trust and respect with the animals. Unfortunately, the ending is quite predictable. Both of them were mauled and eaten.

Application – Do not love the world or anything in the world. Do not get cuddly with the world or its system. And do not get seduced by its power or the false promise of fulfilling all of your desires. Don't build a relationship with a bear. Build a relationship with the One who gives life.

5. The four beasts are four kings (17) – In verse 17, the angel tells Daniel that the four beasts are four kings who shall arise. Each of these kings would establish a new and powerful empire.

Scholars generally agree that the four beasts represent the following four historical nations.

A. The first one was like a lion and had eagle wings – Eagles and lions are both considered to be majestic animals. Eagles are lords of the air and lions are the king of beasts. This beast represents Babylon. Note that its wings were cut off, and it was made to be a man.

This fits with the life of Nebuchadnezzar. He was proud like an eagle. But God humbled him, repeatedly reminding him that he was merely a man and not a god.

Jeremiah also used the images of a lion and eagle in reference to Babylon (Jeremiah 49:19-22).

A winged lion statue taken from Babylon is displayed at the British museum.

B. The second beast was like a bear – This beast appears more carnal than the first. It is pictured as in the very act of devouring flesh. Three ribs protrude from its mouth and it is commanded, "arise, devour much flesh." A bear is slower than an eagle but more powerful.

It represents the Medo-Persian empire and the king who established it, Cyrus. Their armies were notorious for their brutality and strength. Note that the bear was "raised up on one side." That is, one side was larger than the other. Probably this is a reference to the fact that the Persians were more prominent than the Medes.

The three ribs may signify their three great conquests, Egypt, Babylon, and Lydia.

C. The third beast was like a leopard with four wings of a bird and four heads – A leopard is swift but made all the swifter for its four wings.

This beast represents the Greek Empire built by Alexander the Great. He was one of the greatest military minds in history. By the young age of 28, he had already conquered most of the known world. His tactics (four heads) were brilliant and his quick strikes were difficult to repel.

After Alexander died, his kingdom was divided into four parts and split among four of his generals as shown by the four heads of the beast.

D. The fourth beast was dreadful and terrible with great iron teeth – Daniel says that this beast is "different from all the beasts that were before it." The iron teeth remind us of the legs of iron in Nebuchadnezzar's vision of the statue.

The fourth beast represents the Roman empire, which will come in two parts. The first Roman empire was represented by the legs of iron and historically rose to prominence in 27 BC. And the revived Roman empire is represented by the feet of clay and iron and it is as yet a still future kingdom.

The hallmarks of this beast are its strength and ruthlessness. It breaks into pieces and tramples everything that stands in its way.

In addition, it is described as having ten horns, three of which will be plucked out, and a little horn that boasts great things. You can read more on this in our study of Revelation 17 and also later in this chapter.

Application – God knows the future. His sovereign plans come to pass. No man could have predicted the rise and fall of these as yet still future kingdoms so accurately. God can. These last chapters of Daniel remind us that time is in His hands. The future can look terrifying, just as it did for Daniel. But we don't need to be afraid because God is in control.

II. The Ancient of Days reigns (9-12)

Discussion Questions

- Who is the Ancient of Days? Why is He described with this term?
- What are your observations about His appearance?
- What do His clothing and hair teach us about Him?
- What does the fiery fire of His throne signify?
- What might the wheels refer to?
- Describe the heavenly crowd before the throne.
- What was He doing on the throne? Who was He judging?
- What do you think the books contain?
- What was the outcome of the court session?
- How does this passage affect our lives today?

Cross-References

Revelation 19:20 - And the beast was captured, and with it the false prophet who in its presence had done the signs by which he deceived those who had received the mark of the beast and those who worshiped its image. These two were thrown alive into the lake of fire that burns with sulfur.

Psalms 90:2 - Before the mountains were brought forth, or ever you had formed the earth and the world, from everlasting to everlasting you are God.

Psalms 103:19 - The LORD has established his throne in the heavens, and his kingdom rules over all.

Teaching Points

1. The Ancient of Days took his seat on the throne – Daniel uses a unique title for God here. It emphasizes God's eternal existence. One of the major themes of Daniel is the temporary nature of earthly kingdoms contrasted with the eternal nature of God's kingdom.

The words "kingdom," "dominion," "endure," and "forever" appear repeatedly throughout the book as God seeks to teach His subjects that He alone is sovereign and that His kingdom will have no end. Thus the title, "Ancient of Days," is a reminder that long before the beginning of any earthly kingdom, God already existed. He was sitting on His throne before any earthly kings had one, and He will still be sitting on His throne after they are gone.

Application – Remembering who God is and who we are gives us a healthy dose of humility. Next time you question God, remember who was on the throne a trillion years before you were born.

2. His features and the throne room described –

A. His clothing was white as snow – It reminds us of His purity. His glory shines without any blemish.

B. The hair of his head was like pure wool – His white hair shows us His "age." He is the Ancient One, existing from eternity past.

Proverbs 20:29 - *The glory of young men is their strength, but the splendor of old men is their gray hair.*

In addition, his white hair shows His holiness and perfection. We know God is a Spirit. But He chose to manifest Himself to Daniel in this way at that moment to teach us something about His character and essence.

C. His throne was fiery flames – Flames are a symbol of judgment. They also portray refining (like dross eliminated through heat). And again, the fire shows God's holiness. In the Old Testament, when He appeared to Israel, fire was often closely associated. Moses saw the burning bush and God's presence was within the fire. The pillar of fire protected them from their enemies and guided them to their destination. The Shekinah Glory also burned brightly as a fire.

D. Its wheels were burning fire – Thrones on earth generally don't have wheels. It is possible that these wheels represent the mobility of His throne. He is omniscient, observing everything that happens in the entire universe.

E. A thousand thousands serve Him – Every king is served by His subjects. The host of heaven are actively serving the King of Kings. One day, we too will stand serving before Him.

Whereas a thousand thousands serve Him, ten thousand times ten thousand stood before Him. They are standing before Him in judgment. It appears that the number of people being judged is far greater than those who actively serve Him. Unbelievers greatly outnumber the faithful.

F. The court sat in judgment and the books were opened – Every person will stand before God in judgment one day, from the lowest servant to the great kings. Greece's Alexander the Great, Persia's Cyrus, and Babylon's Nebuchadnezzar would all appear before God's throne. He would have the last say. Their high ranking on earth would give them no special favors in heaven. Every person will be judged on the basis of their deeds.

In Daniel's vision, he saw the books opened.

Revelation 20:12 - *And I saw the dead, great and small, standing before the throne, and books were opened. Then another book was opened, which is the book of life. And the dead were judged by what was written in the books, according to what they had done.*

The books record the deeds of men. Judgment will be fair and impartial, based on the evidence.

Application – If Alexander the Great and Nebuchadnezzar cannot escape judgment, do not think that you can. You will be there too, with them facing the Ancient of Days. He sees all and knows all. Are you ready to face your Maker?

3. The results of the judgment – The horn on the fourth beast represents a man who will rule in the last days before this judgment. He will be blasphemous to a point the world has never seen before. Many passages describe his great boasting (Revelation 13:5). This character is widely considered to be the antichrist. The fact that he is connected with the fourth beast shows us that there will be some version of a revived Roman empire in the last days.

Note that at the judgment, this person and his kingdom is the very first one judged. John's description in Revelation matches this one. The antichrist is the very first person judged and thrown into the lake of fire (Revelation 19:20).

One day all of these beasts will be judged. Their dominion will be taken away and Jesus will rule the earth from Jerusalem in the millennium. While the dominion over the earth will be taken away from these nations, people will still exist. Various nations will continue to exist during the millennium.

While various details of these prophecies can be difficult to figure out, the key lessons are clear. The things of this world, including the power of man, are temporary. Small or great, all will stand before God's throne in judgment.

Application – The application of this principle is simple. Imagine two kings asking for your allegiance. You are allowed to see the future. You know one of these kings will reign for a short time and be defeated. Though he makes great boasts, these prove to be lies. The other king will conquer all of his enemies and reign forever. Which one will you ally yourself with? Ally yourself with the King of Kings. Develop your relationship with Him.

III. The Son of Man's kingdom (13-14)

Discussion Questions

- Who is the one like the son of man?
- Why is he called by this title?
- What does this passage show you about the roles of the Trinity?
- How could a man have an everlasting dominion? What hints does this passage give about the nature of Jesus?

- How do you see the theme of kingdoms running through the book of Babylon?
- What key lesson do we learn in this book about kingdoms?
- How is God's kingdom contrasted with man's?

Cross-References

Revelation 1:14-15 - The hairs of his head were white, like white wool, like snow. His eyes were like a flame of fire, his feet were like burnished bronze, refined in a furnace, and his voice was like the roar of many waters.

Mark 14:62 - And Jesus said, "I am, and you will see the Son of Man seated at the right hand of Power, and coming with the clouds of heaven."

John 3:13 - No one has ascended into heaven except he who descended from heaven, the Son of Man.

Teaching Points

1. With the clouds of heaven there came one like the son of man – Son of Man is a title often used by Jesus. The Messianic title signifies the Savior's identity as a man, a representative of the human race. In Scripture, He is often pictured as either going with or coming with the clouds of heaven (Mark 14:62). Daniel has been privileged to see a vision of God the Son in His glory.

2. He was presented to the Ancient of Days – God the Father and God the Son are shown to be distinct.

3. To Him was given everlasting dominion – Here, we see the role of the Father and the Son. The Son voluntarily subjects Himself to the Father's rule. The Father glorifies the Son by entrusting all of creation to His care. Jesus will be the ruler over all. All people of all tribes, nations, and languages will be His subjects. His kingdom will last forever.

Luke 1:33 - *And he will reign over the house of Jacob forever, and of his kingdom there will be no end."*

This prophecy will be fulfilled in Jesus after His second coming and the final judgment (Revelation 19-22).

Application – People generally seek to immigrate to more prosperous countries. There are websites that calculate the value of various countries' passports. Some passports are worth more because the host country is more powerful, has more benefits, or can gain you entrance into more other countries. Therefore being a citizen of Jesus' kingdom is to be desired above everything else! Have you immigrated to become a Jesus' kingdom citizen? Immigration has certain rules before it can take effect. Jesus gives us one. Believe in Him. Do you have faith in Jesus?

IV. Interpretation of the vision (15-18)

Discussion Questions

- Why do you think these visions made Daniel anxious?
- What did he do when he was worried? What lesson can you learn from this?
- What kings might be represented by these four beasts?
- What clues do you see in the beasts' appearance that can link them to specific kingdoms?
- How should a believer react to this vision (18)?

Teaching Points

1. Daniel was anxious and approached an angel – Daniel was a person like you and me. He was not immune to worry or fear. The vision alarmed him. It was terrifying. It is not every day that you see a vision of the end of the world!

Notice what Daniel does with his worry. He immediately goes to seek help. Desiring to find out as much as he could about this vision, he asked someone in the know (perhaps an angel) for an explanation.

Application – There will be many times we are confused or anxious. When you have those feelings, go to the source of all wisdom. There is only One who can solve all of your problems.

2. The interpretation was given to Daniel – Ask and you shall receive. Daniel asked what it meant, and he was told the answer.

The given interpretation is very simple. The four beasts are four kings. Though they have dominion for a time, it is the saints of the Most High who shall receive the kingdom.

Jesus made a similar point in His sermon on the mount.

Matthew 5:3, 5 - *Blessed are the poor in spirit, for theirs is the kingdom of heaven. Blessed are the meek, for they shall inherit the earth.*

Daniel lived in a time when darkness seemed to reign. Judah was defeated. He and his friends were exiles in a strange, foreign land. Idolatry dominated every aspect of culture. Violence, pride, and selfishness were rampant. He needed a reminder that these things were temporary. In the end, God wins. We too need that same reminder. And that is the lesson of Daniel 7.

V. The fourth beast and the antichrist (19-28)

Discussion Questions

- How was the fourth beast different than the others?
- What do the horns on its head represent?
- Who do you think the one horn in verses 20-21 represents?
- What will this person be like?
- How long will he rule (25)?
- What might it mean that he wants to change the times and the law?
- How will this kingdom and ruler meet its end?
- What will happen after the demise of the fourth beast?
- What principles can we learn from this?
- What does this passage teach us about God?
- What does it teach us about man?
- What does it teach us about this world that we live in?
- How important is it to have an eternal perspective?
- How will having an eternal perspective help you resist temptation?
- Based on what we learned in this chapter, shat should your attitude be toward the world?

Teaching Points

1. Then I desired to know the truth about the fourth beast – Daniel's hunger for the truth is commendable. It would be easy to just say, "this is too complicated," and just let it be. But Daniel sought to understand every detail he could.

2. Recap of the fourth beast – In verses 19-22, Daniel recaps what he had already seen in his vision of the fourth beast. It was powerful and brutal. Ten horns were on its head. These ripped out three. And one horn was conspicuous in its boasting. That horn made war against the saints. Finally, the Ancient of Days judged this beast and the saints possessed the kingdom.

3. The explanation –

A. The fourth beast would be different from all the kingdoms.

B. It shall devour the whole earth and trample it down – The Roman empire conquered a vast swath of territory. The revived Roman empire will rule over the whole earth.

C. The ten horns are ten kings – There are many views about these ten kings (see notes on Revelation 17). Some spiritualize these ten kings and say that they refer to the many kings of the Roman empire in history. However, we should take this dream within the context of Daniel. In Daniel 2, the king had a dream of a statue. The statue had ten toes, just like this beast has ten horns. The rock representing the eternal kingdom of God smashed the toes. So Jesus' kingdom will directly conquer this kingdom. That kingdom and Jesus' return are still in the future. Therefore it stands to reason that the ten kings here in Daniel 7 are also still future to us. They will reign over the world in the last days before Christ's return.

At that time, another king will arise, different from them. He will put down three of these ten kings and take dominion for himself. The antichrist will blaspheme the Most High, war against His saints, and even attempt to change time and the law. Notice that time, times, and half a time are given into his hands. That equates to three and a half years, the latter half of the seven-year tribulation period.

Finally, this ruler will be punished. And the true saints of God will partake of His perfect, everlasting kingdom.

Scholars do not agree on every detail of eschatology. Some aspects can be hard to understand. But the key point remains. God wins. Everyone on His team wins. His kingdom lasts forever.

4. Daniel was disturbed by what he saw and heard — God revealed very solemn and weighty events to Daniel. For Daniel's part, he was not apathetic. He cared greatly about the world and what he saw of it through this dream. The Lord clearly held Daniel in high regard to entrust him with these spectacular prophecies.

Amos 3:7 - *For the Lord God does nothing without revealing his secret to his servants the prophets.*

We are blessed that the Alpha and Omega tell us what is to come. He tells us so that we will be ready. Satan attempts to deceive people by promising unending pleasure to those who follow their lusts. God's message is clear. Everything in this world will end. Only His kingdom lasts forever.

Application — Do not be seduced by the short-term pleasures the world offers. Have a long-term perspective.

Daniel 8

Outline

I. The vision of the ram and the goat (1-8)
II. The little horn that took away the burnt offering (9-14)
III. The interpretation of the vision (15-27)

I. The vision of the ram and the goat (1-8)

Discussion Questions

- When did this happen?
- Where was Daniel when he saw this vision?
- What did Daniel see in the vision?
- What are your observations about his vision?
- What were the special features of the ram?
- What were the special features of the goat?
- Why do you think God gave this vision to Daniel?
- What do this vision and its fulfillment show us about God?

Cross-References

Psalm 103:19 - The Lord has established his throne in the heavens, and his kingdom rules over all.

1 Chronicles 29:11-12 - Yours, O Lord, is the greatness and the power and the glory and the victory and the majesty, for all that is in the heavens and in the earth is yours. Yours is the kingdom, O Lord, and you are exalted as head above all. Both riches and honor come from you, and you rule over all. In your hand are power and might, and in your hand it is to make great and to give strength to all.

Psalm 135:6 - Whatever the Lord pleases, he does, in heaven and on earth, in the seas and all deeps.

Teaching Points

Introduction – Daniel chapters 2-7 were written in Aramaic. Chapters 8-12 are written in Hebrew. Daniel's message in these chapters is written primarily to the Jews. He deals with four major Gentile nations. He does not write about everything each nation will do but focuses in general on how the age of the Gentiles affects the Jews and specifically on how they will dominate Jerusalem and the temple.

1. In the third year of the reign of King Belshazzar – The dream came to Daniel after the dream in chapter 7, which occurred in the first year of Belshazzar's reign. At the time, Babylon was in power. Persia was starting to emerge as a power to contend with, but Greece was not yet any type of threat.

2. I was in Susa the citadel – Susa was an important city in the region, the capital of Elam. Later, it would become the capital of the Medo-Persian empire. The backdrop of Esther and parts of Nehemiah take place in Susa.

3. I saw a ram – As Gabriel will explain later in the chapter, the ram represents the kingdom of the Medes and Persians. The ram has long been a symbol of the Persian empire. Persian kings often wore helmets with ram horns in battle. Many aspects of the ram depicted point to specific characters of the Achaemenid Empire.

 A. It had two horns – The empire was forged by an alliance between the Medes and the Persians. Thus, the ram had two horns. Both of these horns were high. Each part of the alliance was strong. However, one was stronger than the other. The higher horn came last. This fits with the fact that the Persian people, who were the stronger part of the alliance, rose to prominence after the Medes.

B. I saw the ram charge westward, northward, and southward – No major conquests were taken by the empire to the east. However, much territory was seized and key battles were fought in the three other directions.

C. He did as he pleased and became great – For a while, the Persian Empire could not be matched militarily. Victories came in all directions. Babylon and Egypt, with all of their history and might, were easily dispatched.

4. A male goat came from the West – In verse 21, Gabriel identifies the goat as representing Greece. Even without this clear statement, with the benefit of history, the goat's identity is clear.

A. Came from the west – Greece started in the west (relative to Israel) and came east.

B. Across the face of the whole earth – This is likely a reference to the vast swath of territories Greece conquered.

Without touching the ground – The Greek expansion was all about speed. Alexander the Great and his armies moved with lightning speed. He didn't stop for long before moving to his next conquest. It was that speed that enabled him to rule such a vast empire by the young age of 31.

C. The goat had a conspicuous horn between its eyes – Most likely, this is a reference to Alexander the Great. His military prowess is legendary. The Greek Empire was established largely because of his genius.

D. The goat struck the ram and broke his horns – The text says that the goat ran at the ram with "powerful wrath." Alexander decisively defeated the Persians in a string of three improbable victories. In each one, the invading Macedonians went against far larger armies. But their superior training, and more importantly, Alexander's tactics, were enough to drive the Persian armies into chaos. The final major battle between the two powers was the Battle of Gaugamela in 331 BC. It was the nail in the coffin of the Achaemenid Empire. Soon after, Darius was killed. Alexander declared himself King of All Asia.

E. The great horn was broken and instead of it there came up four conspicuous horns toward the four winds of heaven - Alexander died suddenly at the age of thirty-one. Because he had not named any successors, his generals divided up the kingdom among themselves with our separate kingdoms emerging.

II. The little horn that took away the burnt offering (9-14)

Discussion Questions

- What does a horn often symbolize in the Bible?
- Which part of the split Greek empire might this little horn come from?
- What does it mean that some of the host and stars of heaven were thrown down?
- Who is this vision describing?
- What does it mean that it became great, even as great as the prince of host?
- What will this person do?
- What is he like?
- Did these things happen already or are they still future?
- What do we learn in this passage about persecution?
- What do we learn in this passage about god's sovereignty?

Cross-References

Psalm 75:10 - All the horns of the wicked I will cut off, but the horns of the righteous shall be lifted up.

Proverbs 16:5 - Everyone who is arrogant in heart is an abomination to the Lord; be assured, he will not go unpunished.

Proverbs 21:4 - Haughty eyes and a proud heart, the lamp of the wicked, are sin.

Teaching Points

1. A little horn – Daniel is still describing the third beast, which represents Greece. The large horn represented Alexander the Great, and the four horns after it were symbols for the four rulers who split the kingdom. In a similar

manner, this "little horn" also represents another ruler within one of these four regions of the split Greek empire.

In chapter 7, there was another "little horn." He made war against the saints and boasted great things. However, that ruler was part of the fourth beast, while the "little horn" in Daniel 8 is part of the third beast. Therefore, although they are very similar in some respects, they are two unique individuals who rule over different kingdoms at different ages.

These two rulers have many similarities. Both hate God and His people. Both desolate the temple. Both trample the Jews. Both are called "little horns." The use of similar imagery is a way God calls our attention to the fact that these two brash rulers are very similar. While ruling over different kingdoms in different eras, they are kindred spirits. Both have the spirit of the antichrist that John talks about in 1 John 4. The first is an antichrist who foreshadows the final most powerful and evil antichrist in the end times.

2. The identity of the little horn – Who is this ruler who will trample God's people?

History reveals to us a ruler who fits the description remarkably well. In fact, he fits it so well that Bible critics refuse to accept that Daniel 8 can be a prophecy and instead try to revise the date of the book.

This historical king is Antiochus IV Epiphanes. He was a Greek Hellenistic king who ruled the Seleucid Empire, one of the four branches of the split Greek empire, from 175 BC to 164 BC.

Antiochus IV took the throne by murdering his brother Seleucus Philopater. He then held Philopater's son and the rightful heir hostage. The name Epiphanes was a name that Antiochus took and it means "illustrious." This name alludes to deity.

Let's look at how this ruler fits the description here in Daniel 8:9-14.

Toward the south, toward the east, and toward the glorious land - Antiochus IV fought the other Greek kingdoms to the south and east in order to expand his territory. In addition, he invaded Palestine (the glorious land) and defeated it.

Some of the host and some of the stars it threw down and trampled them – Daniel is recording a vision and many of the things in the vision are symbolic. Did a man actually grow to the heavens and grab some stars to throw down to the earth? No, that is symbolic language.

We need to ask ourselves what the stars represent.

Sometimes stars represent angels, but that also doesn't make sense in this passage. A man cannot cause angels to fall or defeat angels. However, there is a Bible passage that may shed some light on this.

Genesis 37:9-10 - *Then he dreamed another dream and told it to his brothers and said, "Behold, I have dreamed another dream. Behold, the sun, the moon, and eleven stars were bowing down to me." But when he told it to his father and to his brothers, his father rebuked him and said to him, "What is this dream that you have dreamed? Shall I and your mother and your brothers indeed come to bow ourselves to the ground before you?"*

In Joseph's dream in Genesis 37, the stars are a reference to the tribes of Israel, to Jews. Genesis 15:5 also refers to stars as being Jewish people. Within the context of Daniel 8, this interpretation makes the most sense. Stars refer to Jews.

Antiochus Epiphanes was notorious for his brutal treatment of Jews. In one campaign, he had 40,000 Jews murdered. By some accounts, he was responsible for the death of over 100,000 Jews.

1 Maccabees 1 describes some of the cruelty of Antiochus. He ordered Scripture to be burned and those who possessed it put to death. Parents were forbidden from having their children circumcised. When a child was found circumcised, he was hung and his parents were executed.

The regular burnt offering was taken away and the place of his sanctuary was overthrown – One of his most notorious deeds was the way he desecrated the temple. After a defeat in Alexandria, the despot turned his wrath to Jerusalem. He commanded it to be taken on the Sabbath day. Then he had an image of Zeus erected in the temple. Going even further in his blasphemy, he had a pig sacrificed on the altar.

Because of the desecration, regular sacrifices were stopped.

3. It will throw truth to the ground and it will act and prosper – You might expect that God would immediately intervene and have such a blasphemer summarily struck down by lightning. However, he didn't. Truth was thrown to the ground. And those who did evil prospered. It is not the first time that the wicked seemed to benefit from sin, and it won't be the last.

Asaph questioned why this happens in Psalm 71. Seeing the wicked prosper confused him. How could God allow it? And if that happens, what good is doing the right? Once he meditated on this question, he "perceived their end." He realized that the wicked might prosper for a moment, but in the end, they will be judged. This world is not always fair. But one day, when we face God, everything will be set right.

In His time, God will judge the wicked. But He may tolerate their evil schemes for far longer than we would expect.

Application – Don't be surprised to see the wicked prosper. Neither should you covet their success. Instead, think about where their path will finally lead.

4. The offering and sanctuary will be trampled for 2300 days and then it will be restored –

There are a number of different attempts by scholars to understand exactly the 2300-day part of this prophecy. Unfortunately, some have gone off on this passage and entertained all types of wild speculation and theories. One of these poor interpretations is that each one of these 2300 days signifies a year. William Miller used this theory to espouse the idea that Jesus would return in 1844. His movement was the seed that started the Seventh-Day Adventists and the Jehovah's Witnesses. Obviously, he was wrong.

This prophecy was made in regard to the Greek empire (the goat). It takes place in the days after the splitting of the Greek kingdom. So it would be poor hermeneutics to take these as day-years and extending well past the end of the Greek empire.

Two reasonable interpretations are generally proposed. One is that the "evening and morning" reference is to a 24-hour period. According to this interpretation, it is a total of 2300 days. The other is that it is 2300 evenings and mornings, meaning that it is 1150 total days (each day having one evening and one morning).

We know when the temple sacrifices were restored. After the successful Maccabean revolt, the temple was rededicated on December 25, 165 BC. To commemorate that day, the Jews celebrate Hanukah.

The exact day regular sacrifices stopped is less clear. Antiochus' severe persecution began six years before (fitting with the 2300-day theory). However, the temple was only desecrated about three years before (fitting with the 1150-day theory.)

It is not something that believers should divide over. No matter which interpretation you support, the principle we learn is still the same.

God rules over history. Evil will not be tolerated forever. According to His sovereign purpose, God may allow evil for a time. He allowed Antiochus Epiphanes to set up an image of Zeus in the temple. He allowed a pig to be burnt on the altar. He even allowed His people to be killed. But He did not forget. And He would not allow the evil-doer to go unpunished.

Application – When you look around and see evil triumphing, remember that God will not forget. Neither will He allow it to continue forever. One day He will put a stop to all sin. Each person will face judgment for what He has done. Wrongs will be set right. Do not admire the life of the wicked or the things that he has. Instead, consider what will happen to him and his wealth when God's patience runs out.

III. The interpretation of the vision (15-27)

Discussion Questions

- How did Daniel react when he saw the vision (15)?
- What can we learn from his response?
- What is the desire of the being who looks like a man?
- Who do you think this is? Why?
- What does this teach us about God's desire for us?
- How can we understand the phrase, "the vision is for the time of the end?"

116

- What does verse 24 mean in that this man is powerful, not by his own power? What power?
- How can we guard against becoming great in our own minds?
- How did Daniel react to the vision? Why do you think it affected him so deeply?

Cross-References

Proverbs 25:2 - It is the glory of God to conceal things, but the glory of kings is to search things out.

Amos 3:7 - For the Lord God does nothing without revealing his secret to his servants the prophets.

Psalm 119:30 - The unfolding of your words gives light; it imparts understanding to the simple.

John 15:18 - If the world hates you, know that it has hated me before it hated you.

Matthew 5:10 - Blessed are those who are persecuted for righteousness' sake, for theirs is the kingdom of heaven.

Teaching Points

1. I sought to understand it - A hunger to learn is one of Daniel's outstanding character traits. He didn't just say, "this is too difficult to understand, never mind." He "*sought to understand it.*"

In the twenty-first century, people seem less willing to use their brains. In the age of Netflix binge-watching, some prefer not to use their brain power. It is too tiring. Short attention spans are commonplace. Some statistics tell us that over 50% of people will abandon visiting a website if it takes longer than three seconds to load.

If we are not careful, this mindset can creep into the church. When it does, sermon length grows shorter. And believers continue drinking milk instead of moving on to solid meat.

Hebrews 5:12-14 - *For though by this time you ought to be teachers, you need someone to teach you again the basic principles of the oracles of God. You need milk, not solid food, for everyone who lives on milk is unskilled in the word of righteousness, since he is a child. But solid food is for the mature, for those who have their powers of discernment trained by constant practice to distinguish good from evil.*

Application – When you don't understand something in Scripture, if it is important, seek it out. Study the Word until you find the answer.

2. "Gabriel, make this man understand the vision" – For our part, we are supposed to have a heart to learn. When we do, God graciously teaches us. Throughout Scripture, we see that God has a heart to educate us. He wants us to know the truth. He wants us to see the light. Like a kind shepherd, He leads us step by step. We don't need to walk in the dark.

The Lord opens our eyes and gives us understanding.

Psalm 119:130 - *The unfolding of Your words gives light; It gives understanding to the simple.*

Job 32:8 - *But it is the spirit in man, the breath of the Almighty, that makes him understand.*

It is an amazing blessing for us that our Creator is not only transcendent but also immanent. Immanent is a theological word that means God draws close to us and operates within our world. He is knowable because He has made Himself to be knowable.

Application – Thank the Lord for the light that He gives. And when you are in the dark, ask the source of all light to illuminate.

3. I was frightened and fell on my face – Many Bible characters had the same reaction when they came face-to-face with an angel. They are supernatural, and their appearance can be terrifying.

4. I will make known to you what shall be at the latter end of the indignation – The events of this chapter appear to refer to the Persian and Greek eras of history. These concluded before the time of Jesus. So how can the angel say it is about the time of the end?

Many Bible prophecies have near-term and long-term fulfillment. For example, the Messiah is coming twice. That split fulfillment is not always clear in the Old Testament. The prophecies about the trampling of the temple and the war against the saints seem to be one of these split events with near-term and long-term fulfillment. The first fulfillment can be seen as a foreshadowing of the final fulfillment in the end times. Thus, Antiochus Epiphanes and his cruel treatment of the Jews foreshadow the antichrist who is to come. He is a type of the antichrist to come.

Solomon said in Ecclesiastes that there is "nothing new under the sun," and this is one example of that. The end-times antichrist will, in some way, be an embodiment of all of the evil that has ever come against God's people.

5. Description of the coming king – In verses 23-25, a description is given of this ruler. As noted above, I believe there is a duel-fulfillment of these prophecies.

As Abraham's sacrifice of Isaac was a type foreshadowing Jesus' sacrifice, so Antiochus Epiphanes is a type, giving a hint of the types of cruel persecution God's people will suffer in the last days.

A. A king of bold face who understands riddles – This ruler will be bold and skilled in intrigue.

B. Cunning deceit –He will be very gifted at telling lies. Don't take his words at face value.

C. His power shall be great, but not by his own power – Here is a hint of the evil forces at work behind his rise to power. Satan uses men as pawns in his war against the Almighty. Believers need to prayerfully discern the evil agenda behind men such as these.

D. He shall destroy – His father is the devil and the devil seeks to kill, steal, and destroy (John 10:10).

E. In his own mind he shall become great – This ruler will be pride personified. In reality, he is nothing next to the King of Kings. But he will have his own reality. And in that reality, he is far greater than he actually is.

Application – Let us be reminded not to be great in our minds! Those are qualities of an antichrist. Jesus was humble. Satan is prideful. Whose example are we following?

F. He shall rise up against the Prince of princes and he shall be broken, but not by human hand – Antiochus IV blasphemed the Lord. The antichrist in the end-times will do the same. Revelation 16-19 describes some of the events of Armageddon. Antiochus was struck down with an unknown disease and died. The Maccabees believed this was judgment from God for his desecration of the temple. In Revelation, the beast (the antichrist) will be judged even more clearly. He will be sentenced directly by Jesus and thrown alive into the lake of fire (Revelation 19:20).

Many rise up against God in open rebellion. Many more secretly scoff at Him. God will have the last word. Those who seek to thwart Him will be broken with no remedy.

6. Daniel was appalled by the vision – God had revealed to him some amazing things. No one else alive knew it. It was a heavy burden. But the Lord was gracious. And Daniel was faithful. He was able to continue his duties. Although it seems from Daniel 5 that he did not have active duty at the court during Belshazzar's reign, he apparently was still employed in some capacity.

Application – From this chapter, we see that God holds the future in His hands. He is sovereign and on the throne. Which aspect of your future are you worried about? How can you entrust that to Him? How would your life look different if you entrusted your future to the Lord?

Daniel 9:1-19

Outline

I. Background of Daniel's Prayer (1-2)
II. Daniel's Confession (3-15)
III. Daniel's Plea (16-19)

I. Background of Daniel's Prayer (1-2)

Discussion Questions

- When did this prayer occur chronologically in the book of Daniel?
- What books was Daniel looking at?
- How might he have had access to these books?
- Who wrote the books that Daniel was reading?
- What was Daniel's conclusion about the authority of the books?
- What can we learn from this about the inspiration of Scripture?
- What did he learn from Jeremiah about God's plans regarding Jerusalem?
- How does this passage influence your view of Scripture?
- If Daniel (a prophet) diligently studied the word, then what should we do?

Cross-References

2 Timothy 3:16-17 - All Scripture is breathed out by God and profitable for teaching, for reproof, for correction, and for training in righteousness, that the man of God may be complete, equipped for every good work.

Teaching Points

1. In the first year of Darius – The prayer and the vision recorded in Daniel 9 occur chronologically soon after the fall of Babylon recorded in Daniel 5.

The identity of Darius (mentioned three times in the book of Daniel) is controversial. Modern scholars (who are also critical of the Bible in general) view this figure as fictional. However, the book of Daniel has proved its historical reliability already in the case of Belshazzar. Bible critics also thought that he was a fictitious character until undeniable proof in the form of Babylonian cuneiforms showed that the Biblical account was correct.

Many Bible scholars have studied this issue in-depth. And it goes beyond the scope of this study. Steven Anderson wrote an excellent book with a solution to the identity of Darius the Mede. There are actually two "streams" of history regarding the rise of Persia and its early years. The generally accepted stream is from a historian named Herodotus, and his account is extremely difficult to harmonize with Daniel. However, another ancient historian, Xenophon, has been found to be more reliable in many cases. And his record fits closely with Daniel's.

You can view an article summarizing Steven Anderson's at the link below. Those who are interested in researching it further can read his book.

https://truthonlybible.com/2016/01/08/darius-the-mede-a-solution-to-his-identity/

The Bible has proved itself to be historically accurate over and over again. One day in the future, whether through new evidence coming to light or Jesus' 2nd coming, this fact too will be confirmed.

Application – Faith is the conviction of things not seen. There are some aspects of the Bible that are not 100% proven. However, that doesn't mean that our faith is blind faith. Far from it, our faith is a reasonable faith. Much evidence points to its truth and reliability. For some of this evidence, you can visit answersingenesis.org.

2. I perceived in the books the number of years according to the word of the Lord to Jeremiah –

This is an amazing verse. Firstly, we see that Daniel was a student of the Scriptures. He studied not only the Torah (9:13) but also the recent writings of Jeremiah. Jeremiah was a contemporary of Daniel. His ministry was based in Jerusalem before the first Babylonian conquest of Judah and stretched into the early years of captivity when the last remnants of the land fled to Egypt.

It is likely that Daniel knew of Jeremiah before he was exiled to Babylon. After the first conquest of Jerusalem by Babylon, there were two more. In each subsequent war, more people were taken from Jerusalem to Babylon. At some point, there must have been a copy or copies of Jeremiah's prophecies that were taken to Babylon for the exiles. It should not be surprising that copies were made since Jeremiah had a scribe, Baruch, whose job was just that.

Daniel, as a high-ranking and powerful official, was able to get access to these important scrolls.

We again see Daniel's hunger for learning. He desired to absorb everything He could of God's Word. Like us, he was a Bible student. Though he was a prophet, he could not just direct download anything he wanted from a dream. Though he had far more dreams and visions than the norm, his primary method of learning was still the same as us, studying Scripture.

It was not through a cursory glance that Daniel learned this important prophecy. It must have been through a careful study of Jeremiah's writings.

Note too, that Daniel referred to Jeremiah as a prophet. And he respected his writings as the word of the Lord. Daniel viewed the seventy-year captivity prophecy of Jeremiah as divine truth, not just as speculation.

Application – If the prophet Daniel, who received direct revelation from God, was a student of the word, how much more should we study it? We have much more Scripture available to us now than he did. It is a priceless treasure. When we view Scripture in that way, we will be motivated to dig into it.

3. What did Daniel do after he made this Scriptural discovery? -

He applied it to his life. For him, the prophecy was not just theoretical knowledge. It made a difference in his life. It demanded a personal response. His entire prayer of confession is made as a response to what he had learned in his study of Scripture.

Daniel's example reminds us of the importance of both studying and obeying the word. His model is one of the pillars upon which the theme for this ministry, studyandobey.com, is built.

Application – Every part of Scripture is relevant to our lives. Our job is to first find out its meaning and then apply it to our lives. Do you regularly make changes to your life based on what you learn in the Bible? If not, how can you start?

4. Seventy years must pass before the end of the desolations to Jerusalem –

The prophecy that Daniel references is found in these two passages.

Jeremiah 25:11-12 - *This whole land shall become a ruin and a waste, and these nations shall serve the king of Babylon seventy years. Then after seventy years are completed, I will punish the king of Babylon and that nation, the land of the Chaldeans, for their iniquity, declares the Lord, making the land an everlasting waste.*

Jeremiah 29:10-11 - *For thus says the Lord: When seventy years are completed for Babylon, I will visit you, and I will fulfill to you my promise and bring you back to this place. For I know the plans I have for you, declares the Lord, plans for welfare and not for evil, to give you a future and a hope.*

The prophecies are clear. After seventy years, Babylon would be punished and the exiled remnant would be brought back to the Promised Land again. These prophecies were fulfilled historically after the edict of Cyrus the Great, seen in Ezra 1:2-4.

And it fits with secular accounts of Cyrus' disposition toward conquered enemies.

This inscription was found on the famous Cyrus Cylinder, unearthed by an explorer in 1870. The artifact can now be seen at the British Museum and says,

"I returned to these sacred cities on the other side of the Tigris, the sanctuaries of which have been ruins for a long time, the images which [used] to live therein and established for them permanent sanctuaries. I [also] gathered all their [former] inhabitants and returned [to them] their habitations."

Application – Trust in God's promises. Throughout history, He has been faithful to fulfill what He said He would do, no matter how impossible it looked at the time. Let the example of God's fulfilled promise to restore His people encourage you to trust in His power and goodness today.

II. Daniel's Confession (3-15)

Discussion Questions

- What do you observe about Daniel's attitude in this passage?
- How does fasting connect with prayer?
- What is the significance of sackcloth and ashes?
- How does Daniel view God?
- How does Daniel view himself?
- Why does Daniel frequently use the term "we" while talking with God? What does this show you about his attitude?
- What is the key theme of his prayer?
- What do you learn about confession?
- What sins had the nation committed?
- What had happened to the nation as a result of their disobedience?
- Why is recognizing the consequences of our actions an important aspect of confession?
- Where was this "curse" written in the law of Moses (13)?
- Why is confession so difficult?
- Why is confession so important?
- What do you learn from Daniel's prayer that you can apply to your own prayer life?

Cross-References

Matthew 6:16-18 - And when you fast, do not look gloomy like the hypocrites, for they disfigure their faces that their fasting may be seen by others. Truly, I say to you, they have received their reward. But when you fast, anoint your head and wash your face, that your fasting may not be seen by others but by your Father who is in secret. And your Father who sees in secret will reward you.

Proverbs 28:13 - Whoever conceals his transgressions will not prosper, but he who confesses and forsakes them will obtain mercy.

Ezra 9:6-7 - O my God, I am ashamed and blush to lift my face to you, my God, for our iniquities have risen higher than our heads, and our guilt has mounted up to the heavens. From the days of our fathers to this day we have been in great guilt. And for our iniquities we, our kings, and our priests have been given into the hand of the kings of the lands, to the sword, to captivity, to plundering, and to utter shame, as it is today.

Galatians 6:7-8 - Do not be deceived: God is not mocked, for whatever one sows, that will he also reap. For the one who sows to his own flesh will from the flesh reap corruption, but the one who sows to the Spirit will from the Spirit reap eternal life.

Teaching Points

1. Then I turned my face to the Lord, seeking Him by prayer – Daniel's response to the prophecy was prayer. It drove him to his knees. God had already said He was going to do this. Daniel could have thought, "There is no need to pray. This is a foregone conclusion."

However, he did not view himself (or his people) as a passive observer in God's processes. Instead, he viewed his role as a humble and willing tool to be used by God.

How could God restore Judah if it still didn't repent? Even if He did, how could the Jews survive if they didn't change?

Daniel seemed to believe that confession was necessary before restoration. Or, at the very least, it was a critical part of the *means* by which God brought about this desired *end*.

Application – We are also waiting for a number of God's promises to be fulfilled, most notably Jesus' second coming. There are other prophecies connected to this one, such as the fact that the gospel will be preached to all the nations before Jesus returns (Matthew 24:14). We should not be totally passive spectators simply waiting for whenever. Instead, we should actively pray for his return. And while we are praying, we should seek to win the world for Christ and preach the gospel to all nations. In addition, we should live humble, holy, repentant lives so that we will be ready.

2. With fasting, sackcloth, and ashes – These actions showed Daniel's sincerity and his humble attitude. Sackcloth was a very uncomfortable and coarse fabric that was worn by people who were poor or grieving. In Biblical times, sackcloth and ashes together symbolized extreme mourning, often over sin.

In addition to these visible signs, Daniel withheld himself from food. Fasting allowed him to distance himself from the temporal cares of the world and focus completely on God.

3. And made confession – The key theme in Daniel's prayer is confession. His prayer is quite similar to Ezra's in Ezra 9, and from both we can learn several key ingredients of confession.

A. Daniel starts with praise –

Daniel 9:4 - *I prayed to the Lord my God and made confession, saying, "O Lord, the great and awesome God, who keeps covenant and steadfast love with those who love him and keep his commandments.*

In The Lord's Prayer, Jesus taught the disciples how to pray. He taught them to start, "Hallowed by your name." It wasn't the exact words that were important. Rather, it was the attitude behind the words. God's people are to come before Him with the right mindset, realizing that He is on the throne. He is sovereign over all. We are not to come to Him with demands but instead humbly come to the throne of grace.

Hebrews 4:16 - *Let us then with confidence draw near to the throne of grace, that we may receive mercy and find grace to help in time of need.*

B. Daniel uses personal pronouns "we" and "our" (verses 5, 6, etc.) -

Daniel uses many personal pronouns. He uses "we," "our," and "us." He uses these pronouns even though he wasn't involved in his people's idolatry.

The obvious question is why? Simply put, he is one of the people. He is identifying himself as linked to the group. The prayer would also not seem nearly as genuine if he kept saying how evil the other Israelites were. While he had not committed the sin that led to the exile, he had committed many others, so it was true that the entire nation was guilty in God's sight.

When one wants to confess to God, there should be no blaming or pointing fingers. When people first sinned, Adam pointed to Eve and blamed her, and Eve pointed to the snake and blamed it, but in fact, they were both culpable for the sin they had done (although it was true that they had been influenced by others. The sin of one person or a group can affect the larger body.

Now from God's viewpoint, He clearly does not hold one person responsible for the sin of others. A father should not be punished for his son and vice-versa.

Yet when we come to God in prayer, we should come as the representative of our group (be it America, France, our Bible study group, or our family) and seek God's forgiveness and blessing for the entire group. So here we learn another lesson about confession.

Key principle - True confession takes personal responsibility and doesn't blame others.

C. Daniel had the right view of himself and the right view of God –

We see Daniel's high view of God and accurate view of man throughout this prayer. One example is in verse 7.

Daniel 9:7 - *To you, O Lord, belongs righteousness, but to us open shame.*

There was not a hint of complaint by Daniel. He knew that God was just. Every discipline that they had endured was fair and right. All righteousness was ascribed to God.

Meanwhile, he realized that his people deserved the blame. Their own sinful had led them there.

Application – When confessing sin, humbly come to the throne of grace to receive mercy. Have an exalted view of God and an accurate view of yourself.

D. Daniel realized that their exile was deserved, a just consequence for their sin –

Daniel 9:7 - To the men of Judah, to the inhabitants of Jerusalem, and to all Israel, those who are near and those *who are far away, in all the lands to which you have driven them*, **because of the treachery that they have committed against you**. To us, O Lord, belongs open shame, to our kings, to our princes, and to our fathers, **because we have sinned against you**. To the Lord our God belong mercy and forgiveness, **for we have rebelled against him** and have not obeyed the voice of the Lord our God by walking in his laws, which he set before us by his servants the prophets.

Daniel realized that their exile was a direct result of their sin in God's sight. This doesn't mean that all trials are the result of sin. As we learn in the story of the blind man in John 9, not every affliction is the result of sin. There are many possible reasons for this. But in the case of Israel, God had already told them that He was disciplining them because of their sin. Many times (not always), people's difficulties are the result of poor life choices.

Marriages fail because of sin (of one or other or both sides). A son or daughter won't speak to his parent many times because of the mistakes of that parent. A student fails an exam and misses a chance to enter college because he didn't study hard. A family loses their home and everything they own because of poor financial decisions and getting into too much debt. A person goes to jail because of a lapse of judgment in which he drank too much, drove, and ran over someone. The list goes on and on.

Reflect - Can you think of any examples where your own sin/mistakes caused you a trial or hardship?

Many times, in these types of situations, people would grow bitter. They would complain, get depressed, grow angry at other people, or even lash out at God. This is the wrong response. Instead of blaming others for our problems, we should realize that our own sin has brought us to this low, confess and seek to make right what we have done wrong.

Daniel 9:11 - *And the curse and oath that are written in the Law of Moses the servant of God have been poured out upon us, because we have sinned against him.*

The curse he refers to is most likely a reference to the following from Deuteronomy.

Deuteronomy 28:15 - *But if you will not obey the voice of the Lord your God or be careful to do all his commandments and his statutes that I command you today, then all these curses shall come upon you and overtake you.*

God had warned the Israelites what would happen if they forsook Him. It couldn't have been plainer than what He said in Deuteronomy 28. After that, he warned them repeatedly through the prophets. But they didn't listen. Daniel rightly recognizes it was their disobedience that led to their defeat by the hand of the Babylonians.

Application - True confession realizes that sin comes with consequences. Instead of seeking to shift blame, seek to understand if your own choices are the reason for the trial that you are in.

E. He has confirmed His words which He spoke against us –

The discipline that the Jews faced was not happening within a vacuum. God had clearly warned them ahead of time about what would happen if they rebelled. And they did.

Daniel realized that the consequences were clearly laid out and were 100% fair. The discipline, rather than being a surprise, was actually a confirmation of God's faithfulness. He did what He said He would do.

4. And gained insight by your truth (13) – Daniel views the goal of God's chastening as teaching them an important lesson, one which they hadn't yet learned. It was a very humble attitude to take. If every believer looked at discipline in that light, the church would grow rapidly!

Application – When you face the chastening hand of the Lord, seek to gain insight into His truth in the middle of that situation. God's plans for you have a purpose. If you are in a trial, it is for a reason (Romans 8:28). Never put a good trial to waste! Make sure to learn from it the lessons that God has for you.

III. Daniel's Plea (16-19)

Discussion Questions

- What character qualities of God does Daniel base his plea on?
- What is Daniel's prayer request?
- What quality do you see in Daniel in these verses?
- When does He ask God to do these things?
- What lessons can we learn from Daniel in this passage about prayer?
- Based on what we have learned in this passage, how can you improve your prayer life?

Cross-References

Romans 10:10 - For with the heart one believes and is justified, and with the mouth one confesses and is saved.

Psalm 32:5-6 - I acknowledged my sin to you, and I did not cover my iniquity; I said, "I will confess my transgressions to the LORD," and you forgave the iniquity of my sin. Selah Therefore let everyone who is godly offer prayer to you at a time when you may be found; surely in the rush of great waters, they shall not reach him.

Titus 3:5 - He saved us, not because of works done by us in righteousness, but according to his own mercy, by the washing of regeneration and renewal of the Holy Spirit.

Teaching Points

1. According to your righteous acts – Daniel asks God to act in accordance with His own character. It is hard to argue with that!

Throughout this passage, Daniel acknowledges God's justice in disciplining them the way He did. He knows they deserved it. At the same time, he believes that God is merciful.

A plea for mercy

In verse 17, Daniel says, "listen to the prayer of your servant and to his pleas for mercy." Daniel does not say that he or the nation deserves God's mercy. The definition of mercy is "not getting the punishment that you deserve." He believes God is gracious.

This is the way we are to approach God in prayer. We should not come with demands. We do not come as equals.

Hebrews 4:16 says that we should "approach the throne of **grace**." And Jesus praised the unworthy sinner who humbly acknowledged his own failings to God.

Luke 18:13-14 - *But the tax collector, standing far off, would not even lift up his eyes to heaven, but beat his breast, saying, 'God, be merciful to me, a sinner!' I tell you, this man went down to his house justified, rather than the other. For everyone who exalts himself will be humbled, but the one who humbles himself will be exalted."*

This is the type of prayer that God is pleased with.

Application – How are you approaching the Lord in prayer? Are you coming before Him in humility, recognizing that He is almighty and sovereign over all? God is merciful, but we should ask for His mercy instead of taking it for granted.

For your own sake, O Lord

Two times Daniel asks that God grant his pleas for His own sake (17, 19). He also reminds God that they are His people and called by His name (19).

It is similar to the prayer of Moses in Exodus.

Exodus 32:12 - *Why should the Egyptians say, 'With evil intent did he bring them out, to kill them in the mountains and to consume them from the face of the earth'? Turn from your burning anger and relent from this disaster against your people.*

Moses argues that being harsh with the Israelites would hurt God's own reputation. Punishing them would invite accusations from His enemies.

Daniel is making a similar appeal. They are His people. They bear His name. By acting mercifully toward the nation, God would, in essence, be magnifying His own name. People would see His kindness and glorify Him.

This is, in fact, what is happening. Even today, we study how God restored the Jews to their land after the exile and we praise God for His lovingkindness and faithfulness. And it reminds us that He is also faithful toward us, even when we sin.

2 Timothy 2:13 - *If we are faithless, he remains faithful— for he cannot deny himself.*

Application – Our prayers should reflect a proper understanding of God's nature. If we ask God to go against His own nature or His revealed Word, our prayers are doomed to fail. Therefore we should pray in accordance with His character.

2. Daniel's pleas –

After his confession on behalf of the nation, Daniel makes his request to the Lord.

"Let your anger and your wrath turn away from your city Jerusalem."

"Make your face to shine upon your sanctuary, which is desolate."

"Open your eyes and see our desolations, and the city that is called by your name."

"O Lord, forgive. O Lord, pay attention and act."

In short, he asks for forgiveness and restoration. The seventy years of prophesied exile are nearly over. Daniel pleads with the Lord to restore His people to their land. He asks for God's blessing. And He asks for a blessing on the city of Jerusalem and the "sanctuary" there, which is likely a reference to the destroyed temple.

Daniel's prayers were answered. The books of Ezra and Nehemiah record how God answered this prayer (and surely many more like it) and restored the people. The city was rebuilt. A new temple was erected. And walls were laid.

The story of the exile and return to the land is one of the most amazing in Scripture. Perhaps never before had a people been dispersed like the Jews were and then restored. But as astounding as that was, God would still beat it. After the Roman destruction of Jerusalem in 70AD, the Jews were scattered for nearly 1900 years across the face of the earth. And He restored them again. Time and distance are nothing to God. His promises will always be fulfilled, no matter how impossible it seems.

133

Application – Believe in God's promises. And don't be afraid to ask big things of God. He is a big God.

3. Delay not – Daniel also pleads with the Lord to act quickly. He knew God would move on their behalf, and he hoped this would happen soon.

Application – Based on this passage, what is one practical way you can cultivate a healthy lifestyle of prayer this week?

Daniel 9:20-27

Outline

I. Gabriel brings an answer to Daniel (20-23)
II. The seventy weeks prophecy (24-27)

I. Gabriel brings an answer to Daniel (20-23)

Discussion Questions

- What does this passage teach you about prayer?
- Why was Gabriel sent to Daniel? What does this teach us about God?
- What can you learn from this passage about our Father's heart toward us?
- Why did Daniel describe Gabriel as a "man"?
- What can we learn about the timeline of requests and answers?
- Does God always answer prayers this fast? Why does He sometimes have us wait?
- How does God view Daniel (23)?
- How does this passage encourage you in your prayer life?
- Do you have any testimonies to share about answered prayer in your life?

Cross-References

1 John 5:14-15 - And this is the confidence that we have toward him, that if we ask anything according to his will he hears us. And if we know that he hears us in whatever we ask, we know that we have the requests that we have asked of him.

John 15:7 - If you abide in me, and my words abide in you, ask whatever you wish, and it will be done for you.

Hebrews 11:6 - And without faith it is impossible to please him, for whoever would draw near to God must believe that he exists and that he rewards those who seek him.

Teaching Points

1. While I was speaking and praying – Daniel gave us an excellent example of someone devoted to prayer. This verse implies that Daniel prayed out loud. Praying aloud can be a way to focus better on the words we say. While it is not a rule to pray out loud (God hears even the silent prayers in our hearts), it can help us concentrate as we verbalize our thoughts.

Reflect – What are the benefits of praying aloud rather than silently?

2. While I was speaking, the man Gabriel came to me in swift flight –

Here is one of the fastest answers to prayer recorded in Scripture. Daniel had not even finished his prayer before an answer was hand-delivered to him.

Gabriel is one of the archangels. He often acts as a messenger and brings news or a vision from God to His people. It was Gabriel who told Mary she was going to give birth to Jesus (Luke 1:11-38). Likely Daniel describes him as a "man" because in this case he appeared in the form of a man. Angels can appear in their supernatural form (which generally causes fear to those who see them) or as normal people. The fact that he is not actually a man is made clear since he came in "swift flight," and men can't fly!

3. I have now come out to give you insight and understanding – The heart of God is clearly seen in these words of Gabriel. He wanted Daniel to understand His plans. The heart of our Father toward us is soft and kind. Like a good father seeks to educate and teach his child, so God desires to instruct us. Parents do want their children to grow up ignorant. Neither does God want us to be (Amos 3:7).

Application – Since our Father wants us to know Him and His plan, He has made knowing those things possible. Our job is to treasure His words. We should hunger for that wisdom.

Proverbs 2:1-6 - *My son, if you receive my words and treasure up my commandments with you, making your ear attentive to wisdom and inclining your heart to understanding; yes, if you call out for insight and raise your voice for understanding, if you seek it like silver and search for it as for hidden treasures, then you will understand the fear of the Lord and find the knowledge of God. For the Lord gives wisdom.*

As you hunger for wisdom, you will spend more time studying His Word. And as you study, you will also ask Him to give you insight.

Part of the reason Gabriel was sent is to correct Daniel's misunderstanding of what would happen. Daniel had just studied Jeremiah's seventy-year prophecy. It seems that he believed that Israel's troubles were almost at an end. They would return to the land and then the Messiah would come and establish His kingdom. In essence, Gabriel tells him, "a lot more things have to take place and it is going to take a lot of time."

4. At the beginning of your pleas for mercy a word went out – Here, we get a glimpse into the mechanics of prayer. God immediately heard Daniel's prayer, reminding us that He is omnipresent. It doesn't take a long time for our prayers to reach God. He knows your requests before you even organize your thoughts.

Matthew 6:8 - *Do not be like them, for your Father knows what you need before you ask him.*

Right away, God sets His plan for answering Daniel's prayer in motion. Gabriel says that "a word went out." Presumably, this "word" was from God Himself. Daniel prayed, and God gave a command, ordering Gabriel to deliver His answer to Daniel.

The Lord is the King of Kings. He is on His throne. And He is aware of everything happening in the world and of every single prayer. And sometimes, He personally issues a direct command to the angels in response to our prayers.

It is encouraging to see how God answers prayer. A host of angels are serving Him around the clock, awaiting instructions from their general. At a word, the High King sends them off on various missions of mercy on behalf of His people.

God does not always send an answer so quickly. Sometimes He deems it necessary for us to wait for His response.

Reflect - Why does He sometimes have us wait?

Application – Picturing God as the general in command of a host of heavenly beings can help encourage you when you pray. Do not doubt God's ability to answer your prayer, no matter how big. He has all of the resources in the universe at His disposal. Nothing is too difficult for Him. Believe that He is listening. Believe that He has the power to answer. Believe that He will answer according to what is good for you.

5. You are greatly loved – It is a beautiful reminder of God's love. He greatly loved Daniel. And He greatly loved us as well (John 3:16).

Reflect – How have you experienced God's great love for you?

6. Therefore consider the word and the vision – God sent this message to Daniel. At the same time, Daniel had a role to play. His job was to consider the words and the vision carefully. He should pay careful attention and meditate upon the meaning. It was important for Daniel to use his mind and energy in this process and not be a passive spectator.

II. The seventy weeks prophecy (24-27)

Discussion Questions

- Who and what is this prophecy about?
- Why is the word "decreed" important, and what does it mean?
- What do you think the "weeks" represent? Why?
- What six things would be accomplished during this timeframe?
- What do you think each of these six things refers to?
  - Finish the transgression
  - Put an end to sin
  - Atone for iniquity
  - Bring in everlasting righteousness

- Seal both vision and prophet
- Anoint a most holy place
- When would the "clock" of these seventy weeks start? When did this happen historically?
- What are some of the events that will happen on this prophetic calendar?
- Have any of these things been fulfilled yet?
- Are any of these things still yet future?
- Who is the "he" in verse 27?
- What does this prophecy show us about God?

Teaching Points

1. The seventy-weeks prophecy – This is one of the most detailed and significant prophesies concerning God's plan for history in the Bible. It is essential to understand the context of this prophecy. It is given in response to Daniel's prayer of confession and plea for mercy on behalf of Israel. Daniel had read the prophecy of Jeremiah regarding the restoration of the Jews to Jerusalem. And he was concerned about their apathy, their sin, and their future.

In this prophecy, God told him about what would happen in Israel's future. Note that Gabriel said that seventy weeks were decreed for "your people." Thus, we have a clear indicator that this vision is primarily about God's plan for the Jews. Therefore the "holy city" (Jerusalem) is the focal point for these events.

The literal word in Hebrew, "shavat," translated as "week," means "sevens." It could be used for a day or a year. A literal reading of the text would be, "Seventy 'sevens' are decreed for your people and your holy city."

Almost all Bible scholars agree that the "weeks" are seven-year periods. The total time of this prophecy would then cover seventy times seven years, which equals 490 years. The timeline is split into three sections. The first section is seven sevens, which is 49 years. The second section is sixty-two-sevens, which is 434 years. And the last section is one seven, which is seven years.

It is also important to note that each of these years is only 360 days. The prophetic year in the Bible was 360 days, which is also the number of days used by many ancient calendars. John also counts a three-and-a-half year period as being 1260 days (indicating a 360-day year) in Revelation 11:3 and 12:6.

When accounting for the different number of days used in the prophetic year, we arrive at an approximately 476-year period (for the first 69 weeks).

These three periods of time would cover much of God's future plans for the nation of Israel.

2. The purpose of the seventy weeks – Gabriel lists six things that would be accomplished during this timeline.

They are:

- **Finish the transgression** – This is likely a reference to Israel's apostasy. The worst transgression anyone can commit is to reject God's Son. And this is what the nation of Israel did corporately. In fact, the nation of Israel as a group still rejects Jesus as the Messiah. From Romans 11, we know that one day they will repent.
- **Put an end to sin** – It may be a reference to the final eradication of sin. Or it might refer to Israel's repentance and turning to accept Jesus as their Messiah, thus ending their national sin of rejecting the Messiah. Or it may be a reference to Christ's work on the cross, where He took the payment for sin and conquered it. In every interpretation, the main point is that dealing with sin is integral to God's plan.
- **Atone for iniquity** – A reference to Christ's work on the cross.
- **Bring in everlasting righteousness** – A reference to Him setting up His eternal kingdom. It likely refers to the millennium, which will be established at the end of the final seven-year period.
- **Seal both vision and prophet** – It might mean to fulfill all of the prophecies made here. Since it will be completed and by that time will have already happened, the vision and the prophet will no longer be needed.
- **Anoint a most holy place** – It may refer to the new temple established in the millennium.

Some of these events are easy to understand. Atoning for iniquity clearly references Jesus' work on the cross. Some of the others summarize things that will happen before Jesus' second coming when He sets up His millennial kingdom.

While most of the other visions in Daniel highlight political events and wars, this one shows the spiritual activities which are going on behind the scenes.

Application – God has a purpose for everything He does. His actions are not random. Seeing God's purpose in history reminds us that He also has a purpose for us. Whatever He allows in your life is intended for a specific reason (Romans 8:28). This passage could encourage the nation of Israel and help them remember that even in hard times God loved them and had a plan for them. The same is true for us.

3. The starting point of the "clock" –

The event which started the clock for these 490 prophetic years is the decree to "restore and rebuild Jerusalem."

There are several different decrees which were made by Persian kings in regard to Jerusalem. The most famous one was made by Cyrus

2 Chronicles 36:23 - *Thus says Cyrus king of Persia, 'The Lord, the God of heaven, has given me all the kingdoms of the earth, and he has charged me to build him a house at Jerusalem, which is in Judah. Whoever is among you of all his people, may the Lord his God be with him. Let him go up.'*

However, this decree was that they should go and "build him a house." The order gave the Jews the right to rebuild the temple.

That occurred at about 539 BC. But it wasn't a decree to "restore and rebuild Jerusalem." So we have to keep looking for the starting point.

Another decree was by King Darius to Ezra (Ezra 6:1-12). This law was a re-issuing of Cyrus' decree permitting them to rebuild the temple, which hadn't been completed yet. It occurred in roughly 519 BC.

In Nehemiah 2:1-8, King Artaxerxes issues a decree allowing the Jews to rebuild their city, walls, and gates. The dates of this event are clearly recorded

(Nehemiah 2:1). We know this happened on March 5th of 444 BC (using the first day of the month for when decrees were counted).

Daniel 9:25 NASB - *So you are to know and discern that from the issuing of a decree to restore and rebuild Jerusalem until Messiah the Prince there will be seven weeks and sixty-two weeks; it will be built again, with plaza and moat, even in times of distress.*

After sixty-nine weeks, Messiah the Prince would be "cut off" (9:26).

Going forward sixty-nine 360-day periods takes us to March 30th, 33 AD. Scholars have slight disagreements on when Jesus died. But almost all agree it was between AD 30 and AD 36. The most commonly accepted date is April 3, AD 33. That would put Jesus' triumphal entry to Jerusalem on March 30th, AD 33. The text says, "after the sixty-two weeks an anointed one will be cut off." Amazingly, the numbers line up to the day!

This passage has been instrumental in many Jews coming to Christ as they realized that the Messiah had to historically come at the time when Jesus did!

God is indeed sovereign over history. His plans cannot be thwarted.

Isaiah 14:26-27 - *This is the purpose that is purposed*
concerning the whole earth,
and this is the hand that is stretched out
over all the nations.
For the Lord of hosts has purposed,
and who will annul it?
His hand is stretched out,
and who will turn it back?

Jesus criticized the Jews because they should have recognized it was the time of the Messiah, but many did not.

Luke 19:41-44 - *And when he drew near and saw the city, he wept over it, saying, "Would that you, even you, **had known on this day** the things that make for peace! But now they are hidden from your eyes. For the days will come upon you, when your enemies will set up a barricade around you and surround you and hem you in on every side and tear you down to the ground, you and your children within you. And they will not leave one stone upon another in you, **because you did not know the time of your visitation.**"*

Some did know and recognized it was the time of the Messiah. Simeon seems to be one. But most did not.

Application – God's plans cannot be thwarted. His timing is precise. We can confidently rely on His Word. He has fulfilled it before and He will do so again. If the first 483 years happened as He said (and they did), then the last seven will too! Our faith is reasonable and our hope is sure!

4. The "gap" – The text itself shows there is a gap between the sixty-ninth week and the seventieth week. Take note of the word "after."

Daniel 9:26 - *And **after** the sixty-two weeks, an anointed one shall be cut off and shall have nothing. And the people of the prince who is to come shall destroy the city and the sanctuary. Its end shall come with a flood, and to the end there shall be war. Desolations are decreed.*

Two events are described in verse 26, the cutting off of the anointed one and the destruction of the city and its sanctuary. These events do not take place **in** either the sixty-ninth or seventieth weeks. Rather, they occur **after** the sixty-ninth week but not **in** the seventieth week.

There is a clear gap with *at least* these two events happening in between.

When were the city of Jerusalem and its temple destroyed?

That happened in AD 70 when Rome, under the reign of Titus, destroyed Jerusalem and desecrated the temple. The Jews were once again dispersed throughout the world. So these two events (the crucifixion of Jesus and the destruction of the temple) are separated by 37 years. Therefore there is *at least* a thirty-seven-year gap between the sixty-ninth and seventieth weeks.

But when you look at the events described in verse 27, they haven't happened yet. It stands to reason that the gap is still ongoing. The final seven-year period (described in Revelation as well) has not started yet. We live in the gap. The church age is in the gap.

During the 490 years, God primarily dealt with the world through the nation of Israel. They were, in some ways, the focal point of His work on earth. But during this "gap," God is primarily dealing with the world through His church, which is mainly made up of Gentiles. Over and over again in the book of Acts, Paul said that because the Jews rejected the gospel, he went to the Gentiles.

It is as if at the end of the sixty-nine weeks, a divine whistle was blown. Because the Jews rejected the Messiah, none of the six things listed in Daniel 9:24 were fulfilled yet (that is why the anointed one had nothing). God turned His attention to the vast harvest field of the Gentiles. We are currently in the "intermission" period before He turns His focus back to the people of Israel and the final week of events is fulfilled.

That is why the age we are in now is often referred to as the "last days." We are very nearly at the end of this calendar. We don't know how long it will last. At any moment, God may blow the whistle again, restart the clock, and begin the final week. Once that whistle blows and the clock restarts, it will be only seven years until Jesus returns in glory, having fulfilled all six of the purposes mentioned in Daniel 9:24. Most of the events in the book of Revelation (chapters 4-19) occur within these seven years, often called the "tribulation."

It should not surprise us that there is a gap. The timeline deals with the Messiah and Israel. And the Messiah's career is separated into two parts, His first coming as a Lamb and His second coming as a Lion. In between these two phases of the Messiah's work is the gap year that we see in Daniel and are now living in.

Application – Be ready. We do not know how long it will be until the whistle blows again and the final series of events before Jesus' second coming start happening. We should redeem the time and work as long as we can while it is still day (John 9:4).

5. The final week – There is one seven-year period left in this prophecy that hasn't been fulfilled yet. Some argue that it is actually Jesus making a covenant. But that doesn't make sense for several reasons. One is that it says the people of the prince who is to come will destroy the city and the temple. It was the Romans who destroyed the temple and not the Jews.

In addition, Jesus did not make a seven-year covenant with anyone. Nor will He ever break a covenant like this "prince" does.

The text identifies the "prince" with the people who destroyed the temple. Therefore he must be of Roman ancestry and from the revived Roman empire that we have seen mentioned several times in Daniel's vision already.

What will this person do?

He will make a seven-year covenant with "many," likely a term that refers to the nation of Israel (Daniel 8:25, Revelation 6:1). This peace treaty or covenant will be the time marker that the final seven years have begun.

Halfway through those seven years, he will break the covenant and put an end to the sacrifices and offerings. We see this same 3.5-year reference in Revelation (11:2, 13:5).

Putting an end to the sacrifices implies that there will be a future temple in Jerusalem, and indeed many are working very hard to make this happen. It is the top goal of Orthodox Jews and is supported by over one-third of Jews today. Many of the items for a restored temple have already been made and are being stored for when the temple is finished.

In addition, to stopping the sacrifices, this person will desolate the temple with many abominations.

Jesus mentions this prophecy of Daniel.

Matthew 24:15 - *So when you see the abomination of desolation spoken of by the prophet Daniel, standing in the holy place (let the reader understand).*

Paul also mentions this character.

2 Thessalonians 2:3-4 - *Let no one deceive you in any way. For that day will not come, unless the rebellion comes first, and the man of lawlessness is revealed, the son of destruction, who opposes and exalts himself against every so-called god or object of worship, so that he takes his seat in the temple of God, proclaiming himself to be God.*

The antichrist will go into the holy temple and proclaim himself to be God.

And numerous references are made to him in Revelation. (Revelation 13:11-15).

The antichrist was foreshadowed by Antiochus Epiphanes (175 BC). But the character in Daniel 9:27 is not him. We know this because Jesus talked of him as still being in the future (Matthew 24:15-16).

6. How will it end? –

Daniel 9:27 - *Until the decreed end is poured out on the desolator.*

Gabriel makes it clear that this usurper will be punished. He will be punished exactly as God determines at exactly the time that God determines it.

Truth does not change. And the plan of God that we see in Daniel, we also see in Revelation.

Revelation 19:20 - *And the beast was captured, and with it the false prophet who in its presence had done the signs by which he deceived those who had received the mark of the beast and those who worshiped its image. These two were thrown alive into the lake of fire that burns with sulfur.*

How does it all end?

God wins! That is the comfort for Daniel and the Jewish people. They would endure many trials and tribulations over the centuries. A target would be painted on their backs. But when all is said and done, God's perfect plans for them (Jeremiah 29:11) would come to pass. He wins. And all of those who join His team also win.

Application – Be strengthened in your hope. God's Word will not fail. All that we hope for in the future will one day be a reality. Stand firm and don't compromise with the world. The things we see are temporary and don't last. The things we don't see are eternal.

Daniel 10

Outline

I. The setting for the vision (1-3)
II. A terrifying vision of a man (4-9)
III. Spiritual warfare behind the scenes (10-14)
IV. A personal message of encouragement (15-21)

I. The setting for the vision (1-3)

Discussion Questions

- When did Daniel have this vision?
- What is the "word" he received?
- Why was Daniel mourning?
- What does verse 3 show you about Daniel's character?
- How important is fasting to the life of believers today?

Cross-References

Matthew 5:4 - Blessed are those who mourn, for they shall be comforted.

Isaiah 58:3-7 - Why have we fasted, and you see it not?
Why have we humbled ourselves, and you take no knowledge of it?'
Behold, in the day of your fast you seek your own pleasure,
and oppress all your workers.
Behold, you fast only to quarrel and to fight
and to hit with a wicked fist.
Fasting like yours this day
will not make your voice to be heard on high.
Is such the fast that I choose,

a day for a person to humble himself?
Is it to bow down his head like a reed,
and to spread sackcloth and ashes under him?
Will you call this a fast,
and a day acceptable to the Lord?
"Is not this the fast that I choose:
to loose the bonds of wickedness,
to undo the straps of the yoke,
to let the oppressed go free,
and to break every yoke?
Is it not to share your bread with the hungry
and bring the homeless poor into your house;
when you see the naked, to cover him,
and not to hide yourself from your own flesh?

Joel 2:12-13 - Yet even now," declares the Lord, "return to me with all your heart, with fasting, with weeping, and with mourning; and rend your hearts and not your garments." Return to the Lord your God, for he is gracious and merciful, slow to anger, and abounding in steadfast love; and he relents over disaster.

Teaching Points

1. The third year of Cyrus king of Persia – Chronologically, this takes place after chapter 9 and probably before he was thrown to the lions in chapter 6.

2. A word was revealed to Daniel –

Daniel says that a word was revealed to him and the "word was true." This message appears to be the prophecy in Daniel 11.

Note Daniel 11:2 - *And now I will show you the **truth***.

3. Daniel was serious about the spiritual battle –

In this passage, we will see that there is an unseen spiritual battle raging around us in the world. And Daniel was part of this spiritual battle. His prayers were used by God to accomplish some of the things we see. He was not a passive spectator of this battle. He was part of it. And he was serious about it.

Daniel was a person who lived in the midst of great darkness. Idol worship took place on all sides. His peers schemed politically. The riches of the world and all the pleasures and luxuries he could have wanted were available.

But Daniel did not care for these things. He did not indulge himself in the pleasures of the world. While he lived in the capital of a rich empire, his heart was not there. His heart was set on his people.
Daniel cared deeply for his people. He wanted them to be victorious. And he wanted to know God's plan for his people's future.

Daniel, therefore, engaged himself in a spiritual battle, fighting on behalf of God's people. So what did he do?

He mourns for three weeks. During this time, he fasted from meat, wine, and all delicacies. Verse 12 says that he "*humbled*" himself before the Lord. Daniel sets his heart on fighting this spiritual battle. He doesn't come with weapons. He doesn't come with schemes. He comes with a humble and committed heart. He does not just dabble in and get his toes wet. He doesn't just pray for a few minutes and then say, "my job is done." Daniel commits himself. He is all in. And that requires sacrifice.

Daniel was more than willing to sacrifice for this spiritual battle.

Application: Perhaps there is a serious issue you need to take before the Lord. Are you willing to sacrifice? How committed are you? What are you willing to give up? Serious prayer and fasting require sacrifice. When you take a serious issue to the Lord, you should not just live your life exactly the same and offer a few moments of prayer here or there. We need to humble ourselves before the Lord. We need to focus our whole attention on Him. Like David, we do not come with a javelin. We do not come with weapons of this world. But ours are our spiritual weapons. How serious are you about the spiritual battle in front of you?

II. A terrifying vision of a man (4-9)

Discussion Questions

- Where was Daniel when he had this vision?

- Whom do you think he is describing in verses 5-6?
- What other Bible passage has a description like this one?
- What does the face like the appearance of lightning show you about this person? How about the eyes like a flaming torch? How about his arms and legs like burnished bronze?
- Why was it that only Daniel saw this and those in his group did not?
- How did Daniel react to what he saw?

Cross-References

Acts 9:7 - The men who were traveling with him stood speechless, hearing the voice but seeing no one.

Teaching Points

1. The man in Daniel's vision –

The identity of this being is not given. Some think it is Gabriel or another angel. Others believe it is Jesus preincarnate.

The description is remarkably similar to the one of Jesus in Revelation 1:13-15.

Revelation 1:13-15 - *And in the midst of the lampstands one like a son of man, clothed with a long robe and with a golden sash around his chest. The hairs of his head were white, like white wool, like snow. His eyes were like a flame of fire, his feet were like burnished bronze, refined in a furnace, and his voice was like the roar of many waters.*

His clothing, belt, eyes, arms, legs, and voice are all described similarly.

If it is Jesus, we can make some inferences from the description.

His body was like beryl

Beryl is a mineral that comes in many forms and colors. Some more well-known gemstones that are beryl include emerald and aquamarine.

His face was like the appearance of lightning

It shows his power, holiness, and glory. The vision of His face reminds us that God has the power to kill us instantly. At any moment, He could zap us with lightning from heaven because of our sins. But He doesn't. Instead, He shows us mercy and grace. He is power under control.

His clothing

Leviticus 16:4 – *He shall put on the holy linen coat and shall have the linen undergarment on his body, and he shall tie the linen sash around his waist, and wear the linen turban; these are the holy garments. He shall bathe his body in water and then put them on.*

Hebrews 2:17 – *Therefore he had to be made like his brothers in every respect, so that he might become a merciful and faithful high priest in the service of God, to make propitiation for the sins of the people.*

The clothing is similar to what the high priest would wear. One of the chief roles of the high priest was to come as a mediator between God and man. He offered sacrifices to God, made atonement for sin, and brought God's messages to the people. Now Jesus is our mediator. He is our high priest. He offered Himself as a sacrifice for sins. It is through His work that we can approach the Lord.

In the book of Hebrews, we learn that Jesus is a priest of the order of Melchizedek. It was a unique line different from the Levitical priesthood. Melchizedek was a king and a priest, whereas in Israel, the role of priests and Levites were separate. Jesus also is a priest and a king.

His eyes were like a flame of fire

Jesus sees all and knows all. He has supervision and His gaze penetrates any facade people put up, piercing our innermost thoughts. Nothing is hidden from Him. Instead of thinking that we can keep secrets from Him, we should take "every thought captive" (2 Corinthians 10:5) to Christ.

Application: Think about your own life. What is one "secret" you have that you wouldn't want to be announced in church next Sunday? Take it to Christ. Admit to Him that He knows all. Confess. Bring it to the light. Seek His help to defeat this temptation and He will help you.

Arms and feet like burnished bronze

The altar outside the tabernacle was covered in bronze. Here the bronze is described as "refined in a furnace." It is hot and glowing. Thus it signifies Jesus' holiness. And it reminds us that He is moving through the churches to refine His church.

1 Peter 1:7 - *So that the tested genuineness of your faith—more precious than gold that perishes though it is tested by fire—may be found to result in praise and glory and honor at the revelation of Jesus Christ.*

Throughout Scripture, we see that God uses the furnace of afflictions to purify us. Suffering, trial, and discipline are all meant to refine us, burning out sin and strengthening our faith.

Jesus wants to sanctify His church so that we will become like Him.

Application: Is your life being refined? Share an area of your life that God has been refining lately.

The sound of his words is like the sound of a multitude

In Revelation, John describes his words as like the sound of many waters.

Jesus' voice is both simultaneously powerful, majestic, forceful, peaceful, calming, and gentle. His voice purifies.

Let us look forward to the day when we can hear His wonderful voice with our own ears.

2. Daniel's reaction to the vision –

All of the men who were with Daniel felt something was going on. Fear came upon them, but they didn't know why. Only Daniel saw the vision.

This reminds us that the spirit world is active. It influences the physical world, but many times it does so in unseen ways.

When Daniel saw the vision, he had no strength left. It took everything from him. It is unclear why seeing the vision had such a profound physical effect on Daniel. But we need to remember that spiritual forces are powerful. Daniel had been fighting in this unseen battle for three weeks. He had been fasting and in prayer. Something about the supernatural nature of the vision simply overwhelmed him. It was more than his senses could take.

Perhaps this is why God conceals His full glory from us. Our physical bodies just can't take it.

III. Spiritual warfare behind the scenes (10-14)

Discussion Questions

- Who might have been the messenger that came to Daniel?
- How does he address Daniel? How is this encouraging?
- Why did he come to Daniel?
- How does the phrase "your words have been heard" encourage you?
- What can you learn from Daniel's attitude in prayer?
- What connection do you see between God's answer and Daniel's attitude?
- Who is the prince of the kingdom of Persia?
- What can you learn about spiritual warfare (see also 20)?
- What can you learn about Satan's activity in the world?

Cross-References

Ephesians 6:10-12 - Finally, be strong in the Lord and in the strength of his might. Put on the whole armor of God, that you may be able to stand against the schemes of the devil. For we do not wrestle against flesh and blood, but against the rulers, against the authorities, against the cosmic powers over this present darkness, against the spiritual forces of evil in the heavenly places.

2 Corinthians 10:3-5 - For though we walk in the flesh, we are not waging war according to the flesh. For the weapons of our warfare are not of the flesh but have divine power to destroy strongholds. We destroy arguments and every lofty opinion raised against the knowledge of God, and take every thought captive to obey Christ.

1 Peter 5:8 - Be sober-minded; be watchful. Your adversary the devil prowls around like a roaring lion, seeking someone to devour.

Teaching Points

1. You are greatly loved, fear not –

When God's messenger comes to Daniel, the very first thing he says is that Daniel is "greatly loved." That is a very important message. It did take over three weeks for Daniel to receive a reply. For us, it can take much longer before we see God's answers to prayer. And sometimes, when we look around, it may seem that the other side is winning. When you read the news, it is bad on almost all fronts.

I believe God's message to us is the same as the one to Daniel; we are greatly loved. We must not interpret trials as apathy from God. We can say without a shadow of a doubt that God loves His church, and He loves every person in it. He wants what is best for us. No matter what happens going forward, we must not forget that.

Secondly, the messenger tells Daniel to "fear not." He is told to "fear not" because his words have been heard. God is on his side, not against him. The angel may appear to be quite frightening, but he is on Daniel's side. What does that mean? Daniel's enemies should fear, not him.

The same is true for us. If God is for us, who can be against us?

Reflect – How does knowing you are greatly loved affect you?

2. God answers –

Daniel 10:12 - *Then he said to me, "Fear not, Daniel, for from the first day that you set your heart to understand and humbled yourself before your God, your words have been heard, and I have come because of your words.*

See this. Daniel prayed and fasted for three weeks. During this time, it looked from man's perspective as if nothing happened (in contrast with Daniel 9, when the answer came before he even finished praying). Neither Daniel nor anyone else could see any tangible result from the prayer. But. God heard. God didn't only hear him after three weeks. God didn't only hear him after his prayers escalated to a certain intensity. From the first day, from the very beginning, God heard.

154

And that is a comfort to us. God hears. Every prayer that we make today, God hears. And every prayer that will be made for the rest of this week, God hears. While we should be committed and sacrifice, God's hearing is not dependent on our prayers being perfect. So be confident of this. When you bring your prayers to Him, He always hears.

Secondly, we see that God answered. In fact, God sent the answer right away. As soon as God heard Daniel's prayer, He dispatched an angel to go to Daniel. Some think it was Gabriel, but he is not named here.

Isn't that an exciting thought? God is sitting on His throne. Legions of angels are at His service. When His saints pray, He hears. And God will dispatch angels to the world to help us, fight for us. When you pray, God may say, "Gabriel, go." [Or another angel].

How will God respond to your prayers? When you raise your voice to God, He hears. How will He answer? We don't know exactly how, but we know that He will!

Application – Pray in confidence, knowing that God hears and will answer.

3. Satan opposes –

But that is not the end of the story. We just saw God heard. And answered. But the result was not seen right away. The messenger God sent runs into some trouble.

And here is a fascinating behind-the-scenes look at the spiritual battle raging around us. The angel who was sent as a messenger to Daniel could not come. For three weeks, he was stopped. Opposed. Who would dare oppose him?

Daniel 10:13 – The prince of the kingdom of Persia withstood me twenty-one days.

Who is this? It is a powerful demon. This demon appears to be assigned by Satan to the kingdom of Persia. It is his job to influence that kingdom in favor of Satan. You see, Satan is staking his claim over this land. He wants to keep it in the dark. And so he sends his own forces to blind men, to influence kings, shape politics, and oppose God's forces.

And we see many of the results of these demonic forces in the book of Daniel. Some truly terrible laws are passed. One time a law was passed that every person must worship an idol or be thrown into a fire. Another time a law is passed that all people must pray to the king only for 30 days. These are evil laws. And they have an evil origin. From this passage, we can see that Satan's forces are at work in this kingdom. And it is reasonable to conclude that laws like these were spawned from his own mind. His fingerprints are all over them.

Satan is opposing God. He opposed him then. And he does so now. He uses politics, laws, and governments to enact his policies and fight against God. And note that this demon is not a weakling.
For three weeks, he was able to successfully resist this angel and slow him from his mission.

What lesson can we learn from this?

Satan is opposed to God's work. And he will use every means at his disposal to fight, including spiritual forces and including government, politics, and laws.

Satan has not stopped working since the book of Daniel was written. He is still active. As he tried to influence the world at that time through politics, so he continues today.

Application - We need to be aware that we have an enemy. We need to be aware that this enemy works through people and systems. He seeks to influence governments, laws, schools, universities, media, and more to forward his sinister schemes. The devil wants to enslave you and put you in chains. And thus, we need to know that coming to God for help is our only solution. We must depend fully on Him. We are unable to win this battle ourselves. Even the angel in this passage needed help! We certainly do as well.

4. God's forces win, but sometimes it takes time –

Satan opposed God. Demonic forces were fighting angelic forces. But now for the good news. It took three weeks, but God won. When the first angel ran into opposition, Michael came. God's forces win.

Revelation 12 depicts the unseen cosmic war of the ages between God and Satan. In the end, God wins.

God has a plan for you. It might not be what you expect or hope. But He is going to win and the result will be good for you.

We get the wonderful privilege of being part of the process. As we draw near to Him in prayer, He will draw near to us. You are not to be a spectator but are part of the battle.

Application - So, let us be patient to wait for God's answer. At the same time, joining this battle requires sacrifice. Diligent prayer requires sacrifice. What are you willing to sacrifice as you come to God in prayer? For Daniel, it was luxury and meat for three weeks.

Let us look forward with hopeful expectation to see what God will do on our behalf when we humble ourselves before Him. Because we know He wins.

IV. A personal message of encouragement (15-21)

Discussion Questions

- What "vision pains" did Daniel refer to?
- Why did he lose all strength?
- How did the messenger respond to Daniel's weakness?
- How many times did Daniel need to be strengthened just to continue this conversation?
- What does the response of the messenger show you about God's heart toward His children?
- What did you learn about prayer that you can apply to your life this week?
- What did you learn about spiritual warfare that you can apply to your life this week?

Cross-References

Isaiah 41:10 - Fear not, for I am with you; be not dismayed, for I am your God; I will strengthen you, I will help you, I will uphold you with my righteous right hand.

1 John 4:18 - There is no fear in love, but perfect love casts out fear. For fear has to do with punishment, and whoever fears has not been perfected in love.

Ephesians 6:10 - Finally, be strong in the Lord and in the strength of his might.

Teaching Points

1. Daniel strengthened twice – The awesome vision Daniel took in began to overwhelm him again. Firstly, he could not summon the strength to talk and was mute. Someone (it is not always clear in the passage who is who) touched his lips and he was able to speak. With his first words, he described his own weakness. He had no strength to even carry on in a conversation.

He was touched again and strengthened a second time saying, "*O man greatly loved, fear not, peace be with you; be strong and of good courage.*"

The angel (or Jesus) did not blame Daniel for his weakness. Instead, we see compassion and mercy toward Daniel, although he was clearly physically inferior. Our Lord sympathizes with us (Hebrews 4:15) rather than judging us.

Application – Firstly, we should thank God for His compassion. He graciously gives us strength when we have none. He picks us up when we are down. Secondly, His compassion should motivate us to show the same care to others. When others around you are weak, do you also seek to strengthen them? Or do you look down on them for their weakness? If we are to be like Jesus, then we must treat others with mercy.

I never could understand things like America's Funniest Home Videos. They would show clip after clip of people falling or hurting themselves, and the audience would laugh. Rather than laughing when people fall, let us help them up.

After Daniel was strengthened, he was ready to hear what the messenger had to say.

2. I will return to fight against the prince of Persia and when I go out, behold, the prince of Greece will come –

The spiritual warfare wasn't constrained to just a three-week period. It was ongoing. And it took place in other parts of the world too, not just Persia.

What we see here is an amazing behind-the-scenes look into the spiritual world that Paul alludes to in Ephesians 6:10-13. Satan continuously seeks to influence the world and advance his evil schemes. God's warriors are sent to respond. They fight against these demons and hold evil at bay.

Can you imagine how evil the world would be if God stopped holding back the tides of darkness and just abandoned us?

2 Thessalonians 2:6 - *And you know what is restraining him now so that he may be revealed in his time.*

The Lord, His angels, and His church acts as a restraining influence on the excesses of wickedness.

Application – You are part of God's plan. You are a warrior in His army. What is your role in this battle? How can you fight against these spiritual forces of wickedness?

3. I will tell you what is inscribed in the book of truth – Chapter 11 is an account of this. Daniel 10 details the personal interactions of Daniel, his prayer, vision, and encounter with the heavenly messenger. For the actual contents of that revelation, join us in studying Daniel 11!

Daniel 11

Outline

I. The rise and division of Greece (1-4)
II. Back and forth between kings of the north and kings of the south (5-20)
III. The contemptible king (Antiochus IV) and his wars (21-35)
IV. The far fulfillment: antichrist (36-45)

I. The rise and division of Greece (1-4)

Discussion Questions

- What is the main content of Daniel 11 about?
- What does the fulfillment of such detailed prophecies teach us about God?
- Why did the angel share these prophecies with Daniel?
- Why was it important for the Jews to know these things were going to happen?
- Who is "I" in verse 1?
- Who is the mighty king in verse 3?
- How was verse 4 fulfilled in history?

Teaching Points

1. Overview of the chapter – This chapter contains perhaps the most detailed prophecy in Scripture. It covers a period of around 375 years with stunning accuracy and precision. And the last parts of the prophecy point to the end times and the final war over Jerusalem.

The prophecy starts off with Persia. Then it moves to Persian aggression against Greece, the Greek invasion of Persia, the splitting of the Greek kingdom into four parts, and the centuries-long war between the Ptolemy and Seleucid empires.

The prophecy is so accurate that atheists refuse to accept the traditional date for the writing of Daniel. Since they don't believe in God, they cannot believe that these prophecies were made before the fact. Therefore they date the book of Daniel over four hundred years later to a time after these events were already history. It should be noted that they do so without evidence, simply believing that it is impossible that this could have been written before the events happened.

But God controls time and history.

He knows the future better than we know the past. – David Guzik

The farther we go back in the past, the murkier our memories get. God exists outside of time. It should not be a surprise to us that He can accurately predict the future. He is sovereign over it!

Isaiah 46:9-10 - *Remember the former things of old;*
for I am God, and there is no other;
I am God, and there is none like me,
declaring the end from the beginning
and from ancient times things not yet done,
saying, My counsel shall stand,
and I will accomplish all my purpose.

Prophecies like Daniel 11 remind us of God's sovereignty.

Application – Knowing that God is sovereign over the past, present and future encourages us in the following ways:

- Faith – Since he has proved Himself to be faithful and His promises to be sure in the past, He will do the same in the future. The prophecies that have not been fulfilled yet (such as His second coming) will be. We can take it to the bank.
- Perseverance – Knowing that God is sovereign over history encourages us to persevere. We are not subject to ill luck or random chance. Instead, God is working behind the scenes for our good. He wants to accomplish His perfect plan in our lives. Therefore, we should persevere and not give up.

161

- Hope – We have great hope for the future. The world will not end through some chance disaster such as an asteroid or a nuclear war. Something even better than what we have now is coming.
- Boldness – One of the key themes in Daniel is that God is on the highest throne. His kingdom endures forever. These prophecies remind us that worldly powers will not last. The person who is sitting in judgment toward you will himself be judged. The one who claims authority over you, himself has an authority. You do not need to fear man. Boldly do what is right without compromise because all will answer to the Lord one day.

2. In the first year of Darius the Mede, I stood up to confirm and strengthen him – In this verse, "I" is the angel. The angel is speaking. The statement gives us another behind-the-scenes look at the spiritual realm. One of the tasks of this angel was to influence the king of Persia. The events of Daniel 11 probably occurred around three years after the decree for the Jews to return to the land. Here we see that an angel on a mission for God was instrumental in influencing the king in making this decree and in showing kindness toward God's chosen people.

3. Three more kings shall arise and a fourth shall be richer than all of them… He shall stir up all against the kingdom of Greece –

The fourth king of Persia mentioned here was Xerxes I (486-465 BC). His invasion of Greece is well-documented. Xerxes organized one of the largest armies ever mustered in the ancient world. Initially, he had some victories. But at the Battle of Salamis, his army was defeated. Finally, he was forced to retreat. Greece got the upper hand and later would counter-attack and invade Persia.

4. A mighty king shall arise – Scholars agree that this mighty king refers to Alexander the Great.

The Jewish historian Josephus records an amazing encounter between Alexander and the high priest. Alexander often allowed his army to ransack cities he conquered. But before he came to Jerusalem, he had a dream. In his dream, he saw the high priest and others coming out of the city to him in white garments.

When he approached the city, the dream was fulfilled. The high priest actually showed Alexander the prophecies in the book of Daniel concerning a mighty Greek ruler who would conquer Persia. Alexander the Greek took this to refer to himself. He was so pleased that he offered sacrifice to God according to the high priest's direction. He believed it was a sign from God of his coming victory. And so, Alexander spared Jerusalem and continued his conquest of the Persians.

For a detailed account of this story, read Josephus, Antiquities of the Jews, book XI, chapter 8: https://penelope.uchicago.edu/josephus/ant-11.html

5. Verse 4 –

Daniel 11:4 - *And as soon as he has arisen, his kingdom shall be broken and divided toward the four winds of heaven, but not to his posterity, nor according to the authority with which he ruled, for his kingdom shall be plucked up and go to others besides these.*

Alexander's kingdom was divided into four parts upon his early and untimely death. However, it was not passed to his "posterity." Alexander had no child and no heir. The kingdom instead went to four of his generals.

II. Back and forth between kings of the north and kings of the south (5-20)

Discussion Questions

- Who are the kings of the south?
- Who are the kings of the north?
- Where was Jerusalem in relation to these two kingdoms?
- What kind of things do you see taking place in this chapter?
- What are the things that motivate the key players in these events?
- What does this show you about the nature of man?

Cross-References

1 Timothy 6:10 - For the love of money is a root of all kinds of evils. It is through this craving that some have wandered away from the faith and pierced themselves with many pangs.

Teaching Points

1. The kings of the south and the kings of the north –

Alexander's kingdom was divided into four parts. Two of these kingdoms were neighbors of Israel. One of them was to the south (and west) of Israel. And one was to the north. Therefore these titles are given from the perspective of Israel. Israel was wedged right in the middle, caught between a rock and a hard place.

The "kings of the south" refer to the Ptolemaic dynasty in Egypt. And the "kings of the north" refer to the Seleucid dynasty in Syria.

2. Back and forth fighting for centuries – Verses 5-20 record centuries worth of detailed prophecies regarding the long-lasting back-and-forth war between these two kingdoms. Many scholars have carefully examined these prophecies and found them to be fulfilled in incredible detail.

Alliances

Daniel 11:6 - *After some years they shall make an alliance, and the daughter of the king of the south shall come to the king of the north to make an agreement. But she shall not retain the strength of her arm, and he and his arm shall not endure, but she shall be given up, and her attendants, he who fathered her, and he who supported her in those times.*

Daniel 11:17 - *He shall set his face to come with the strength of his whole kingdom, and he shall bring terms of an agreement and perform them. He shall give him the daughter of women to destroy the kingdom, but it shall not stand or be to his advantage.*

Alliances were made but subsequently broken.

War

Daniel 11:7 - *And from a branch from her roots one shall arise in his place. He shall come against the army and enter the fortress of the king of the north, and he shall deal with them and shall prevail.*

The wars mentioned in Daniel 11 cover over 200 years. One side would hold the advantage for a while, and then the other side. Each side sought to win dominion over its enemy.

Plunder

Daniel 11:8 - *He shall also carry off to Egypt their gods with their metal images and their precious vessels of silver and gold, and for some years he shall refrain from attacking the king of the north.*

Rebellion

Daniel 11:14 - *In those times many shall rise against the king of the south, and the violent among your own people shall lift themselves up in order to fulfill the vision, but they shall fail.*

Jews who were aware of the prophecies in Daniel would seek to rebel against the Ptolemaic dynasty, but they would fail.

Conquest of Israel

Daniel 11:16 - *But he who comes against him shall do as he wills, and none shall stand before him. And he shall stand in the glorious land, with destruction in his hand.*

The glorious land is a reference to Israel. This prophecy was fulfilled when Antiochus III the Great took dominion over Israel. After this point, Israel was under Seleucid rule.

Insolence and Pride

Daniel 11:12 - *His heart shall be exalted.*

Daniel 11:18 - *Afterward he shall turn his face to the coastlands and shall capture many of them, but a commander shall put an end to his insolence. Indeed, he shall turn his insolence back upon him.*

In these verses, we see a clue as to the motivations of these kings. They are prideful and insolent. Their ego spurs them to greater conquest and victory. Continual war was not good for their subjects. Countless people died. The kings cared not. Their tables were filled with delicacies. And the actual battles were fought by others. Nameless multitudes of people died to satisfy their unquenchable egos.

Absent from this story is any desire to seek God's will.

Proverbs 9:10 - *The fear of the Lord is the beginning of wisdom.*

Proverbs 4:7 - *The beginning of wisdom is this: Get wisdom.*

These ruthless rulers did not fear God. And they had no desire to seek wisdom. They were motivated by money, power, and conquest. God's chosen people were stuck in the middle and paid the price.

Taxes

Daniel 11:20 - *Then shall arise in his place one who shall send an exactor of tribute for the glory of the kingdom. But within a few days he shall be broken, neither in anger nor in battle.*

How are all wars funded? Taxes!

3. Key lesson - God sometimes "shows off" by showing us what is going to happen in such incredible detail that it must be from Him and not from man.

Passages like this magnify the Lord and remind us of the supernatural inspiration of Scripture. No man can do what He does.

2 Peter 1:21 - *For no prophecy was ever produced by the will of man, but men spoke from God as they were carried along by the Holy Spirit.*

III. The contemptible king (Antiochus IV) and his wars (21-35)

Discussion Questions

- Who is the contemptible person in verse 21?
- What do you observe about his character?
- What do you learn from verse 27 about the two kings?
- What does verse 28 mean that "his heart shall be set against the holy covenant?"
- What will happen in the new invasion against Egypt (30)?

- How would this leader react to his defeat (30-31)?
- How does verse 32 encourage the Jews at that time?
- How does it encourage all believers who face trials and persecution?
- How can believers be strengthened to stand firm?
- How does knowing God help one to stand firm?
- How did God use the persecution for good (35)?

Teaching Points

1. A contemptible person will come in without warning and obtain the kingdom by flatteries –

Scholars agree that this vile person is Antiochus IV. He was not heir to the throne. His older brother, Seleucus III, was king. Seleucus III was assassinated. Many suspect Antiochus IV was responsible as he assumed the throne soon after. As the text says, Antiochus IV engaged in extensive flattery with relevant parties to win their favor.

Antiochus IV gave himself the title Epiphanes, which means "illustrious." Many Jews instead called him Epimanes, which means "madman."

2. The character of Antiochus IV –

Daniel 11:21 describes him as contemptible (some translations say, "vile.")

The rest of the chapter paints a very ugly picture of this wicked man. Here are some of his character qualities:

- **Flatterer (21)** – He was skilled in intrigue and smooth speech, using it to his advantage.
- **Deceiver (23)** – Alliances he made were just a mask for him to carry out his sinister purposes.
- **Wicked (27)** – The text describes him as "bent on doing evil." Many politicians have evil motivations and desires but attempt to cover them up. With Antiochus IV, there was little façade.
- **Treacherous (27)** – He would sit down and feast with his enemies, pretending to make alliances and deals. But his words were lies and he never intended to carry them out.

3. His defeat by the Roman fleet at Kittim (30)

167

Though he continued to wage war against Egypt, he couldn't completely master it. Egypt finally called for help from Rome. And it is this defeat that verse 30 describes.

"In a famous battle, the Roman Navy defeated the navy of Antiochus Epiphanes. After the battle, a Roman general drew a circle around Antiochus in the dirt and demanded to know if he would surrender and pay tribute to Rome – and demanded to know before he stepped out of the circle. From that point on, there was no doubt: Antiochus Epiphanes took his orders from Rome and was under Roman dominion."

Source - https://enduringword.com/bible-commentary/daniel-11/

After being defeated by the combined Roman and Egyptian forces, Antiochus was furious. As he retreated back through Judah, he took out his wrath on the Jews.

4. Antiochus Epiphanes persecuted the Jews (28-34) –

Daniel 11:30 - *For ships of Kittim shall come against him, and he shall be afraid and withdraw, and shall turn back and be enraged and take action against the holy covenant. He shall turn back and pay attention to those who forsake the holy covenant.*

History tells us that he had 80,000 Jews killed, 40,000 enslaved, and 40,000 taken prisoner. Here are some of the worst acts he committed:

- Parents who circumcised their sons were hung along with the circumcised child.
- The temple was desecrated.
- The altar was desecrated when he had a pig sacrificed on it and sprayed pig blood around the temple.
- An image of Zeus (Antiochus IV was Greek) was set up in the temple.

His anger about his failures to subdue the Ptolemies was taken out on the Jews, whom he seemed to have an extreme disdain for. The persecution he doled out on the Jews gave rise to the Maccabean Wars.

5. Encouragement to God's people in the midst of darkness –

In the middle of all of this war, death, destruction, and persecution is a beautiful verse of encouragement.

Daniel 11:32 - *But the people who know their God shall stand firm and take action.*

It was a dark time for the Jews. They had been caught in the middle of two warring empires for two hundred years. The two sides played tug-of-war over Jerusalem. But now they were the main target. Persecution and trials seemed to go on and on without end. What hope did they have against such powerful (and wicked) kingdoms?

This verse could give them courage. Those who know God would be strengthened by Him. It certainly includes knowing God's plans and prophecies. It also includes knowing how all of this would end, with God victorious.

But to know God goes beyond having theoretical knowledge of God's plans. It means to have a relationship with Him. It means to know His character, power, and goodness. Strength to carry on in the face of persecution would not come from alliances, wealth, or sheer power. No, they were not to rely on the same weapons of war that their enemies did. Their strength came from their relationship with God. The closer they were to Him, the stronger they would be.

Their faith would enable them to stand firm and not compromise in the face of persecution. And if they had faith in God, He would also help them take action. Taking action might be a reference to the Maccabean revolt and their hard-won freedom from the Seleucids.

Application – The same principle is true for us today. If we know God, we too can stand firm and take action. Much of the world is trending toward a direction that is less welcoming toward Christians. Persecution in many countries is increasing.

That persecution is not always in the form of torture, imprisonment, or death. Sometimes it takes the form of cultural or economic persecution. You may be fired from your job if you don't accept your company's worldview. You may be ostracized in the community if you don't go with the flow in supporting their anti-Christian ideals.

Your strength to stand firm should not come from conservative news outlets or political discussion boards. It should come from a deep, personal relationship with the Lord. When you know the outcome (see Revelation and the return of Jesus as the triumphant king), it gives you hope and strength. And when you know God, you know He has a perfect plan for you. You know He will never leave or forsake you. And you know that the Holy Spirit is within you, and will give you the courage you need to stand firm just when you need it (Mark 13:19).

More than just knowledge, a personal relationship with the Lord will give you the inner strength, resolve, and peace to do what is right even when the whole world is going the other way (Exodus 23:2).

6. God is doing a refining work among His people –

Why did God allow these things to happen to His chosen people? He could have stepped in and stopped the persecution immediately. But we see a glimpse of His divine purposes in verse 35.

Daniel 11:35 - *And some of the wise shall stumble, so that they may be refined, purified, and made white, until the time of the end, for it still awaits the appointed time.*

Persecution is one way in which the Lord brings about character growth. Like a fire refines by exposing impurities for removal, trials purify believers.

Reflect: What are some ways that trials purify believers?

IV. The far fulfillment: antichrist (36-45)

Discussion Questions

- What are the characteristics of the king described in 36-39?
- What figure does this seem to be describing?
- What religion would this king have?
- What would he put his trust in?
- How would he recruit more people to his side (39)?
- When will the final battles starting in verse 40 take place?
- Do you think these things have happened yet? Why or why not?
- What will this person do to Israel (41)?

- How will all of this end (45)?
- What key lessons can we learn from this chapter?
- How does knowing the end encourage us today?
- If the leader who puts his trust in money and power ends up like this, what should our attitude be toward those things?

Cross-References

Revelation 13:5 - And the beast was given a mouth uttering haughty and blasphemous words, and it was allowed to exercise authority for forty-two months.

Revelation 19:20 - And the beast was captured, and with it the false prophet who in its presence had done the signs by which he deceived those who had received the mark of the beast and those who worshiped its image. These two were thrown alive into the lake of fire that burns with sulfur.

Isaiah 40:8 -The grass withers, the flower fades, but the word of our God will stand forever.

Teaching Points

1. A shift from short-term to long-term fulfillment –

Many Biblical prophesies have a short-term and long-term fulfillment. The near-term fulfillment is often smaller in scale and points to the long-term event as the ultimate climax. It is something like a person looking at two mountain peaks that are lined up. Although the one closest to him is lower in altitude, because it is closer, he only sees that one. Only after scaling that mountain could he see the larger mountain peak ahead. If you were in the valley between these two peaks, you could see both but would be aware that the farther mountain was taller.

That is the situation we are in now. Antiochus IV Epiphanes was a type of the antichrist to come. He was *an* antichrist, foreshadowing *the* antichrist still to come. As such, he had many of the same characteristics of the final antichrist, who would display them on a larger scale.

While Antiochus IV desolated the temple, the antichrist will go even further.

While Antiochus IV was prideful, the antichrist will be more so.

While Antiochus IV set up an image and demanded worship of Zeus, the antichrist will take the next step, set himself up above all gods, and demand worship of himself.

The text says that these things will happen in the "latter days" (Daniel 10:14).

Paul also describes these events as still future.

2 Thessalonians 2:3-4 - *Let no one deceive you in any way. For that day will not come, unless the rebellion comes first, and the man of lawlessness is revealed, the son of destruction, who opposes and exalts himself against every so-called god or object of worship, so that he takes his seat in the temple of God, proclaiming himself to be God.*

Satan has used similar methods throughout history. Solomon said, "there is nothing new under the sun." The end-times, one-world dictator will be like Antiochus IV reloaded.

2. He shall magnify himself above every god and shall speak astonishing things against the God of gods –

While Antiochus IV did not respect God, he did not turn away from his country's own gods. He was loyal to the Greek pantheon. This statement will be more clearly fulfilled in the antichrist, who is oft-described in Scripture as being highly blasphemous and demanding worship.

3. He shall prosper until the indignation is accomplished –

Daniel 11:36 - *He shall prosper till the indignation is accomplished; for what is decreed shall be done.*

A time limit is enforced on the antichrist. He will not be allowed to rule indefinitely. God will only permit him to reign for a very limited amount of time (3.5 or 7 years; see Revelation).

That is good news for all the followers of God! God remains sovereign. He will still be in control and sitting on the throne of thrones.

Application – Do not be discouraged. God's purposes will be accomplished. While he does permit evil for the time being, it is on a short chain. He will have the last say. Knowing that should give us hope even in the darkest times.

4. He shall pay no attention to the gods of his fathers or the one beloved by women –

One school of thought is that this means he is a Jew (and turns away from Judaism) and homosexual (doesn't care for the love of women).

However, a simpler reading is that he will not be religious at all. No matter what country he comes from, he will reject the traditional faith of that country as he will exalt himself above all gods and demand mankind's devotion and worship.

And the one "beloved by women" is likely a reference to the Messiah (Haggai 2:7).

5. He shall honor the god of fortresses – This tyrant will trust in power. He will be all about war and military might.

6. The final war – Verses 40-45

These verses appear to be describing still future events in the end-times shortly before Jesus' second coming.

7. Yet he shall come to his end with none to help him – As is often said, these prophecies can be simply summarized as "God wins!"

Over the course of history, many have rebelled against God. Some gained greater power and some gained less. Some ruled longer and some had shorter reigns. All will come before the throne of judgment and give an account for their every word and deed.

The Antichrist will be the most powerful ruler the world has ever seen. His kingdom will literally be a world empire and span the entire globe. Many will follow him and give their worship and fealty. But in the end, all will abandon him. No one will be able to rescue him out of God's hands.

Reflect – How does knowing God wins influence your life and decisions now?

173

Application – Do not trust in or pursue the things of this world. They are temporary and will fade away. Only the things of God are eternal. What is one specific way you can pursue the things of God this week?

Daniel 12

Outline

I. A time of trouble and the final resurrection (1-4)
II. The time of the end (5-12)

I. A time of trouble and the final resurrection (1-4)

Discussion Questions

- Verse 1 says, "at that time." At what time?
- What is Michael's relationship with Israel?
- What is the "time of trouble?" How will this trouble be different from any other in history?
- What will be the end result for the Jews?
- What book is referred to (1)?
- What does it mean to "sleep?"
- What can we learn from verse 2 about the resurrection? Who will resurrect?
- How does knowledge of the future resurrection influence your life now?
- In what ways are the wise like stars?
- How can you shine like a star in your culture? Your neighborhood? Your family?
- What does it mean for Daniel to shut up the words and seal the book? Until when?
- What does the phrase "many shall run to and fro, and knowledge shall increase" mean?

Cross-References

Revelation 12:7 - Now war arose in heaven, Michael and his angels fighting against the dragon. And the dragon and his angels fought back.

Matthew 24:29 - Immediately after the tribulation of those days the sun will be darkened, and the moon will not give its light, and the stars will fall from heaven, and the powers of the heavens will be shaken.

Revelation 20:4-6 - They came to life and reigned with Christ for a thousand years. The rest of the dead did not come to life until the thousand years were ended. This is the first resurrection. Blessed and holy is the one who shares in the first resurrection! Over such the second death has no power, but they will be priests of God and of Christ, and they will reign with him for a thousand years.

John 11:25-26 - Jesus said to her, "I am the resurrection and the life. Whoever believes in me, though he die, yet shall he live, and everyone who lives and believes in me shall never die. Do you believe this?"

John 6:40 - For this is the will of my Father, that everyone who looks on the Son and believes in him should have eternal life, and I will raise him up on the last day."

Philippians 2:15 - That you may be blameless and innocent, children of God without blemish in the midst of a crooked and twisted generation, among whom you shine as lights in the world.

Teaching Points

1. At that time – This refers back to Daniel 11:40, which says "at the time of the end." Daniel 11 gives an overview of what the Jews would face in the future. First, they would face hundreds of years of trials, turmoil, and war. A vile person (Antiochus IV Epiphanes) would dominate and persecute them. He was a foreshadow of an even worse antichrist to come. The prophecy then zooms forward from the time of Antiochus IV to the "time of the end," which is still yet future to us. The seventieth week (the final seven years) of Daniel's prophecy is still yet to happen. In those seven years, the antichrist will rise up and take world dominion. It will be a "time of trouble" like none before.

2. Michael shall arise – Michael is one of the chief archangels. Here his role as protector of the Jews is revealed. Here we see a glimpse behind-the-scenes

into spiritual warfare. Angels are members of God's army. As their commanding general, He assigns them missions. Michael's mission would be related to protecting the Jews. Presumably, God sends many angels around the world to different countries with unique missions.

God's assignment of Michael to the Jews at the time of the end shows us that He is not finished with them yet. He still has amazing things in store for them. Other passages (Romans 11:26-27, Revelation 11:13, Zechariah 13:8-9) teach us that God still plans to save a large number of the Jews in the future. It is a reminder of God's grace. Though the people of Israel have rebelled against the Lord many times in the past and rejected God's own Son, He always preserves a remnant. Ultimately, He will restore the nation as a group (though not every individual) to Himself. Thus, while Satan will be working through the antichrist to carry out his plans, God will not be absent. He will be bringing His plan for His people to fruition.

3. There shall be a time of trouble, such has never been –

The "time of trouble" is often referred to as the "tribulation."

Jesus mentioned this frightening time in Matthew 24:21 –

For then there will be great tribulation, such as has not been from the beginning of the world until now, no, and never will be. And if those days had not been cut short, no human being would be saved. But for the sake of the elect those days will be cut short.

The tribulation is also known by other names in Scripture, including The Great Tribulation (Matthew 24:21), "Time of Trouble," (Daniel 12:1), "Jacob's Trouble" (Jeremiah 30:7), "Great and Terrible/Awesome Day of the Lord" (Joel 2:31).

The seven-year period will be divided into two parts. While the first part may be relatively peaceful and prosperous, the second half will begin with the abomination of desolation and things will go downhill quickly.

Revelation paints a bleak picture. Intense persecution will come upon all believers as they will refuse to follow the antichrist. War, famine, and disease will run rampant. But the trouble will go beyond man-made disasters. God will pour out a series of twenty-one supernatural judgments upon the world that will be living in open defiance of Him. Some of these will include earthquakes, oceans turning to blood, hail, poisoned water supply, extreme heat, extreme cold, and boils (Revelation 6-16). The scale, intensity, and frequency of disasters will be worse than anything the world has ever seen before. For those alive during that time period, it will feel as if the world is ending (because it is).

Joel tells us that these things will conclude with the return of the Lord.

Joel 2:31 - *The sun shall be turned to darkness, and the moon to blood, before the great and awesome day of the Lord comes.*

Reflect – Why will God release these judgments and increase the trouble facing the world at that time?

4. But at that time your people shall be delivered – This statement gives hope! All is not lost.

God's purposes run deep. While He will bring these plagues upon the world in order to judge it, that is not the only reason. The Lord will use these events for great. They will act as a wake-up call to many. Each plague will be a warning that worse is still to come upon those who continue to live in rebellion. Together with the judgments, an invitation to repent will go out. Through angels (Revelation 14), two special witnesses (Revelation 11), and 144,000 evangelists (Revelation 7), the light will still shine. And because the darkness will be darker than ever before, so the light will shine brighter.

Hard-hearted people do not change their minds and trust in God easily. The Lord will use these plagues to wake people up and shock them out of their apathy. Few, if any, agnostics will remain. Battle lines will be drawn. Everyone will be forced to take a side.

And God's people shall be delivered. Daniel must have been encouraged to hear this promise. Though Israel would face terrible trials over the centuries, God would not abandon them. In the end, His divine purpose is for her salvation. Huge numbers of Jews will be saved (Revelation 7). And these, in turn, will bring the gospel to the world as untold multitudes of Gentiles from every tribe and tongue will turn to the Lord (Revelation 7:9-12).

Application – Remember God's faithfulness. Even in the darkest storms, He has a divine purpose. All things work together for good to those who love Him (Romans 8:28). The tribulation will be a frightening and painful time. And yet God will use it to bring salvation to millions. In like manner,

178

God desires to use trials in your life for good. Diamonds are made through intense heat and pressure. Our Father does not seek to use trials to overwhelm us but to refine us and to create something beautiful. So when you face trials, don't despair. Trust in the Lord and remember that His love never fails. Every one of God's good promises to you will be fulfilled.

Joshua 23:14 - *Not one word has failed of all the good things that the Lord your God promised concerning you. All have come to pass for you; not one of them has failed.*

5. Final resurrection –

There will be two resurrections. The first is a resurrection to life and the second is a resurrection to eternal punishment.

Daniel 12:2 – And many of those who sleep in the dust of the earth shall awake, some to everlasting life, and some to shame and everlasting contempt.

The second resurrection is described in Revelation 20:12-14. It consists of unbelievers of all ages who are gathered forth to the Great White Throne and then sentenced according to their deeds.

The first resurrection occurs in stages. It includes Jesus as the firstfruit, the promise of what is to come.

1 Corinthians 15:20 – But in fact Christ has been raised from the dead, the firstfruits of those who have fallen asleep.

The second stage is the resurrection of the "dead in Christ." These will be raised at the rapture.

1 Thessalonians 4:16 – For the Lord himself will descend from heaven with a cry of command, with the voice of an archangel, and with the sound of the trumpet of God. And the dead in Christ will rise first.

And the third and final stage is seen in Revelation 20:4.

Revelation 20:4 - *They came to life and reigned with Christ for a thousand years.*

Many believe that this life is all there is. I have asked scores of people what they believe will happen after death and some of the most common answers include "nothing" or "I will turn into dust."

Believing that there is nothing after death is one of the greatest mistakes a person can make.

Reflect – How does one's belief about what happens after death shape their life now?

A person who does not believe in life after death will also not believe in judgment. Where there is no accountability or authority, a person will do whatever he likes to do. This person will desire to live his best life now. He will live for the moment. Self will be his king. Pleasure will be his pursuit. In the end, such a person will die without leaving behind anything of eternal value. Whatever he has earned or achieved will rot, rust, or fade away. Such a life is empty and meaningless.

But God did not create us to live this way. He gave us a soul. We are made in the image of God. And though we don't exist for eternity past, our souls will exist in eternity future. The decisions we make in our life on earth will affect not only our eternal destiny but others as well. Our choices have eternal consequences. That means that the life we live during our short time on earth is packed with meaning and purpose.

Application – Therefore, don't waste your life! Firstly, make sure your faith is placed in Jesus so that you can take part in the blessed resurrection. Secondly, invite others to do the same. Thirdly, live your life for Jesus, building His kingdom, because that has eternal value.

6. Those who are wise shall shine –

The world will get darker and darker as the end times approach (2 Timothy 3:2). Against a dark backdrop, lights shine brighter. We live in the midst of a crooked and perverse generation and so do we. Our mission from the Lord is to "shine as lights." Jesus told the disciples that He is the "light of the world" (John 8:12.) Another time, He said, "you are the light of the world" (Matthew 5:14.)

God calls us to be wise Christians, followers of Christ. We are to live differently than the worldly people around us. Instead of pursuing materials, money, fame, achievement, and pleasure, we pursue Christ. He is our authority. He is our standard. He is our pearl of great price.

We are to live life according to the wisdom from above, not worldly wisdom (James 3:17).

The world is falling head over heels into relativism, which evil teachings like evolution only contribute to. Similar to the time of the judges, people do what is right in their own eyes. Traditional standards of right and wrong are being eroded before our eyes as people celebrate sin in many forms. Sin is not only tolerated, but it is promoted. And those who condemn it are labeled as bigots and are persecuted.

Against this backdrop, those who follow Christ live in stark contrast to the world. When we uncompromisingly follow His standard, we shine His light to a lost world. No, we don't walk around with actual halos. But our actions show people a better way, the Creator's way. The Word of God is a lamp to our feet and a light to our path, leading people in the right way. In a similar way, your actions can lead people to God.

Let us seek to "turn many to righteousness!"

Application: If a neutral observer had unrestricted access to watch you live your life 24/7, would they conclude that you are much different from an unbeliever? Would they know you are a follower of Christ only through observing your actions?

7. Shut up the words and seal the book until the time of the end –

There are three (or more) interpretations of this statement. One is that "shut up and seal" means to keep the book's contents secret. It is hard to reconcile this interpretation with the fact that the contents of the book of Daniel are not secret.

Did he disobey? Did he keep it secret for a while but then release it (though the command is to shut it up until the time of the end)? Did he keep some other part of it secret?

It does not seem that Daniel kept the book secret since we are reading it today.

The second interpretation is that this command means to preserve the book and keep it safe. To "shut up the words" of the book could mean that it is complete and should nothing should be added or taken away from it. A similar instruction is given to John at the end of the book of Revelation (Revelation 22:18). And to seal the book could mean to preserve it, keeping it safe for all generations to read.

In other words, the revelation was now finished. Daniel could put down his pen. From that point, his job shifted to one of preservation. The knowledge in his book would be needed throughout the ages, including the end times.

The second interpretation seems to make more sense. God revealed these things to Daniel for our benefit and the benefit of all believers through time.

A third interpretation is that Daniel was to share the vision with others "as is." He wasn't to go to great lengths to share the interpretations with others because it wasn't yet time to do so. As time passed and events unfolded, things would become clearer according to God's timing.

8. Many shall run to and fro and knowledge shall increase –

Some take this to be a general prophecy about the world in future times. They believe it might refer to world travel (or even space exploration) and a general increase in physical knowledge. One cannot die that travel and knowledge have increased exponentially in the last two hundred years.

However, reading this verse in context shows that there is a simpler and more reasonable interpretation. The Hebrew word for "run to and fro" refers to a person searching for something. Because Daniel preserved the prophecy, wise people in the end times will search his book for answers about God's plans. As world events turn sour during the tribulation, even more people will be sent to Daniel's writings in an attempt to make sense of what they will be seeing and to know what would happen next.

As people do that, "knowledge shall increase." One purpose of the book of Daniel is to give insight and understanding to God's people in regard to God's plan. Also, as time passes and more of God's plan is revealed, the prophecies in Daniel will become easier to see and understand. Knowledge of these end-time events will increase.

Application – Like the Bereans in Acts 17:11, we should look through the Scriptures as a lens for understanding the world we live in. Our desire should be to grow in the knowledge of the Lord and His plans. To do that, we need to study!

II. The time of the end (5-12)

Discussion Questions

- What others do you think Daniel saw?
- What are your observations about their size?
- What do you think the time, times, and half a time represent?
- How did the angel respond to Daniel's further questioning in verse 8?
- Why do you think the angel gave this answer?
- According to verse 10, how would people react to these things during the tribulation?
- What will happen to start this "clock?"
- What do you think will happen at the end of the 1335 days?
- We have seen how many things end. What would the end be for Daniel?
- (See the end of this lesson for several book-in-review discussion questions).

Cross-References

Romans 11:26-27 - And in this way all Israel will be saved, as it is written,
"The Deliverer will come from Zion,
he will banish ungodliness from Jacob";
"and this will be my covenant with them
when I take away their sins."

Revelation 7:9, 14 - After this I looked, and behold, a great multitude that no one could number, from every nation, from all tribes and peoples and languages, standing before the throne and before the Lamb, clothed in white robes, with palm branches in their hands. 14 I said to him, "Sir, you know." And he said to me, "These are the ones coming out of the great tribulation. They have washed their robes and made them white in the blood of the Lamb.

Revelation 22:10-11 - And he said to me, "Do not seal up the words of the prophecy of this book, for the time is near. Let the evildoer still do evil, and the filthy still be filthy, and the righteous still do right, and the holy still be holy."

Teaching Points

1. Two others stood – Most likely, it refers to two angels.

2. It will be for times, time, and half a time – This is likely a reference to three-and-a-half years, half of the length of the final seven-year period. The same time frame is seen in many other Scriptures (Daniel 7:25, 9:27, Revelation 11:3, 12:6, 12:14, 13:5).

3. The shattering of the power of the holy people comes to an end – Israel will be trampled and crushed throughout its history, but especially in the great tribulation. The final battle before Jesus' second coming will be against the holy city. It and its people will be overcome. The Jewish nation will have lost all power and be on the verge of total annihilation when Jesus returns and wipes out her enemies (Zechariah 14).

4. What shall be the outcome of this? – Daniel is hungry to learn more. However, this time the angel tells him, "*Go your way, Daniel, for the words are shut up and sealed until the time of the end.*"

To paraphrase, "Enough questions, Daniel. God has given you everything He is going to for now." The revelation God gave Daniel was nearly complete. Many of Daniel's questions had been answered. But not everything would be revealed until the time of the end. That is going to make everything more clear.

5. Verse 10 –

Daniel 12:10 - *Many shall purify themselves and make themselves white and be refined, but the wicked shall act wickedly. And none of the wicked shall understand, but those who are wise shall understand.*

In the end times, many people will be saved. Revelation 7:9-12 describes a vast multitude of believers from across the world worshiping the Lamb. They will be in white clothes, purified by the blood of Jesus.

184

However, not everyone will be saved. Many will ignore the Scripture. They will not respond to the clear signs of the times. They will scorn warnings to repent and instead pursue a lifestyle of sinful pleasure. There will be a widespread delusion as people are influenced by demonic forces and refuse to place their faith in God, whose existence will be undeniable.

6. There will be 1290 days after the burnt offering is taken away – It is a very specific prophecy. The clock will start on the day the burnt offering is taken away (for this to happen, the temple will first be rebuilt and daily sacrifices reinstituted). One thousand two hundred sixty days is equal to 3.5 three-hundred-sixty-day years. It is also a number used elsewhere to describe half of the tribulation period (Revelation 11:3, 13:5).

So there are three different numbers of days given that are related on this eschatological clock; 1260, 1290, and 1335.

Scholars agree that Jesus will return 1260 days after the mid-point of the tribulation when then the sacrifices are stopped in the temple. The other two numbers are less clear.

Many believe that judgment upon the survivors in the world will begin on the 1290th day and will last forty-five days. On the 1335th day, the millennium will commence under Jesus' newly established kingdom. Hence, the angel says that the one who makes it until the 1335th day is blessed. Only believers who "pass" the judgment would then enter into the millennium.

7. Go your way till the end – Daniel had been given spectacular revelations. His mind must have been racing with so many terrifying and awesome thoughts about the future. He was given a simple instruction to go and do what he should do until the end of his life. The revelation, as exciting as it was, did not change what Daniel was supposed to do on a day-to-day basis. He was to serve God faithfully by obeying and continuing to be a positive influence in society.

Application – Studying prophecy is exciting. We should study it and seek to understand it. But neither should we have our heads in the clouds. God calls us to ready ourselves for Christ's return by living holy lives, obeying His Word, and sharing with others about Him. God gave Daniel a ministry in Babylon. And He has given you a ministry as well. Be faithful to fulfill it every day of your life right up until the last second when your time on earth is up.

8. You shall rest and stand in your allotted place –

One day, after his time on earth was up, Daniel would get to rest. But it wasn't yet time for him to rest. As long as his breath remained, there was still work for him to do.

Hebrews 4:9-10 - *So then, there remains a Sabbath rest for the people of God, for whoever has entered God's rest has also rested from his works as God did from his.*

The same is true for us today. One day we will rest. That rest will be similar to the way God "rested" on the seventh day after He completed creation. It will not be a total absence of work. Rather, our mission on earth will be completed. We will have eternal rest in Him.

Application – Now is not the time for us to rest. We are called to work for the Lord as long as we can (John 9:4). As long as you have breath, your work for the Lord on earth is not done. What is God calling you to do? What still remains unfinished?

At the same time, knowing there is rest for us in the future encourages us to persevere now.

Book In Review Discussion Questions

- Summarize the key theme of Daniel in one sentence.
- What is the most memorable passage for you in our study of Daniel? Why?
- Which principle, verse, or idea has had the biggest impact on your life?
- Going forward, what application do you hope to make based on what you learned in the book of Daniel?

Final Note

If you enjoyed this study on Daniel, visit our website at studyandobey.com for more inductive Bible studies like these.

Made in the USA
Middletown, DE
18 January 2023

22510444R00106